Kickstart Your Motivation

Kickstart Your Motivation

The Complete Guide to Challenging Yourself to Win

Sue Stockdale

JOHN WILEY & SONS, LTD

Other Wiley Editorial Offices

John Wiley & Sons, Inc., 605 Third Avenue,
New York, NY 10158–0012, USA

WILEY-VCH Verlag GmbH, Pappelallee 3,
D-69469 Weinheim, Germany

John Wiley and Sons Australia Ltd, 33 Park Road, Milton,
Queensland 4064, Australia

John Wiley & Sons (Asia) Pte Ltd, 2 Clementi Loop #02–01,
Jin Xing Distripark, Singapore 129809

John Wiley & Sons (Canada) Ltd, 22 Worcester Road,
Rexdale, Ontario M9W 1L1, Canada

British Library Cataloguing in Publication Data

A catalogue record for this book is available from the British Library

ISBN 0–470–84384–5

Typeset in New Caledonia by Florence Production Ltd, Stoodleigh, Devon.

Printed and bound in Great Britain by Biddles Ltd, Guildford and King's Lynn.

This book is printed on acid-free paper responsibly manufactured from sustainable
forestry, in which at least two trees are planted for each one used for paper
production.

Contents

About the Author   ix
Acknowledgements   xi

Chapter 1   Where Does Motivation Come From?   1
             Messages that Shape Our Beliefs   8
             Encouragement Reaps Rewards   9
             The Value of Role Models   10
             The Role of Mentors in Encouraging
                 Motivation   11
             Taking Responsibility for Our Own Success   13
             Recognizing the Company Values   14
             Summary   16

Chapter 2   Testing Your Capabilities   19
             The Opportunity   22
             Using Information to Minimize Risk Taking   24
             Enthusiasm is the Key Ingredient   25
             Building on Success   28
             Using Passion to Make Fund-raising Easier   29
             Overcoming Fear   32
             Preparation and Planning   34
             Flexibility is Key to Survival   36
             Team Issues   39
             Stepping Out of Our Comfort Zone   42
             Managing a Changing Environment   44
             Feeling Invincible   46
             Summary   48

Chapter 3   Building on Success   51

What Happens to Integrate Learning?   53
Harnessing Motivation to Benefit Both the
        Individual and the Company   55
Helping Others to Help Yourself   56
Using Intuition in Decision Making   62
Effects of Fear on Behaviour   65
Being True to Your Values and Beliefs   68
Summary   70

Chapter 4   The Ultimate Challenge   71

Inhibiting Factors   76
Negative Motivation Can Work Too   77
Making a Commitment   78
Selecting the Team   79
Raising the Bar   84
Targeting Companies for Funding   86
Effective Preparation and Planning   87
Team Development   88
Physical Fitness   94
Mental Strength   96
Addressing the 'What if' Scenarios   98
Summary   100

Chapter 5   Stepping into the Unknown   103

Using Expert Knowledge to Anticipate
        Potential Problems   111
Goal Setting   113
Routine Can Help People to Feel
        Comfortable and Safe   117
Valuing Diversity   119

The Gender Question   121
Leadership   124
Autocratic Style   126
Democratic Style   126
Learning to Survive with Less   129
The Mental Mindset   131
Maintaining Focus   134
The Dangers That May Appear on Your
    Journey Towards your Goal   135
Being Aware of How Your Behaviour
    Impacts on Others   137
Summary   139

Chapter 6   Reaching the Pole   141

Combating Complacency   143
Fast-forming Teams   149
Summary   154

Chapter 7   Been There, Done That, Now What?   155

Future Thinking   157
Taking Control   159
The Ingredients for Success   162
Using your Intuition   164
Rising to the Next Challenge   167
Grasping Opportunities   169
The Power of a Vision   172
Being an Inspirational Leader   174
Managing Failure   175
Communicating Your Message Effectively   182
Summary   185

Chapter 8	Winning	187
	Searching for a Deeper Meaning	189
	Finding your Niche	191
	Achieving Goals	192
	Summary	196

References	197
Recommended Reading	199
Useful Contacts	203
Index	208

About the Author

Sue Stockdale is an international motivational speaker, people performance specialist and workshop leader as well as an accomplished polar adventurer. She holds a Masters Degree in Quality Management and Improvement and is studying for an MBA in Entrepreneurship and Business Venturing.

She was the first British woman to walk to the Magnetic North Pole, and also represented Scotland in 3000-metre and cross-country running. Sue is MD of The Human Dimension Ltd and uses her diverse experience to provide a truly unique service as a business expert helping organizations and people to improve their performance and achieve their goals.

Speaking events and workshops can be booked through Cunningham Management UK (0044) 208 233 2824.
Email: info@cunningham-management.co.uk
Website: http://www.suestockdale.com

Acknowledgements

To Jan and Roger for providing the perfect writing environment

To Bronco for offering support, advice and encouragement

For the numerous people who have played a part in helping me to
archieve my goals

Chapter 1

Where Does Motivation Come From?

In this chapter we examine:

- The qualities of peak performance
- The value of role models and mentors
- Company values and their impact on people

ometimes in our careers, we are full of enthusiasm and energy and feel we can face anything that life will throw at us. At other times, we get jaded, lose focus and lack motivation to achieve anything meaningful. Wouldn't it be great if we understood more about what affected our motivation and how it could be harnessed to ensure that more of us are motivated for longer at a time to achieve what we want!

This book is designed to help you do just that. It is a story to provide inspiration about the amazing things we can achieve in our careers and our lives when we are motivated. It is also a guide with simple easy-to-follow lessons that enable the reader to take the meaning from challenging situations that have occurred in some of the most extreme environments in the world and apply this learning to your own journey towards achieving your goals.

You *can* do whatever you want, be whatever you want, and achieve whatever you want. What it takes is to understand and challenge your own beliefs which impact on your level of motivation, and then harness the most powerful part of your body – the brain – to listen to the messages that you *choose* to program it with, rather than the ones that it takes in from other people and your subconscious mind.

If you choose to take control of your brain and the messages you tell yourself, then your life may never be the same again. It does not matter if you are 15 or 55 years old, the principles are just the same. We can learn to become personally empowered, capable of withstanding the pressures of life and work, and able to bounce back even though things get tough.

At the heart of this approach lies the concept of *Learned Powerfulness*™. This concept was developed by Dr Alan Beggs and Graham Williams in 1999 to encompass the three key elements that contribute to peak performance: *Focus, Authenticity* and *Resilience.*

Think of any peak performer in sport, business or adventure. They all possess the following qualities to varying degrees:

Focus – They focus on what they want to achieve in the future and have a high level of awareness
Authenticity – They ensure that their goals are in alignment with their true values and beliefs.
Resilience – They are able to withstand the emotional knocks in life.

Focus – Think what happens when you are not focused on what you want to achieve. Competing priorities get in the way, and we can end up being very productive but not moving towards our goal. In business this can be seen in people who are always very busy but never seem to achieve anything. Energy needs to be focused and in order to achieve this, you need to be aware of what is happening in the present to help or hinder your progress towards your goal. In my own experience of working in a small company, time can often be spent firefighting problems for other people and if you are not careful then time runs out during the day and the key tasks that were meant to be achieved are not done. A weekly review of progress against targets can help to overcome this problem by keeping you focused on what the priorities are.

Authenticity – Being true to your values is also critical otherwise you might end up in the situation of being a vegetarian working in an abattoir! In business this can cause problems when the goals and values of the company do not align with your own personal values.

I experienced this when I worked on a contract with the United Nations Protection Force for a year in the former Yugoslavia. My role was to improve the efficiency within the civilian organization, and in the short term it appeared to be possible, but after several months it became obvious to me that while those at the top said they wanted to be more efficient, their actions did not live up to the rhetoric.

For example, senior staff would arrange for us to work with a particular department to improve the way it operated, and when we presented the report outlining our findings and suggesting some changes, the report would mysteriously go missing, or the head of the department would then explain all the reasons as to why our recommendations could not possibly be implemented. This was particularly noticeable when the recommendations involved reducing staff numbers or suggesting that UN employees were not skilled enough to carry out the tasks they were meant to be doing.

In the end I decided not to renew my contract because the role I was trying to perform (to improve efficiency) did not match with the organization's behaviour, when it appeared to me that there were too many people with too much at stake to be willing to reform or improve efficiency. These decisions are tough ones to make, but being authentic and living your values is not always an easy road.

Resilience is the third quality that peak performers have. They are able to withstand the tough times and can bounce back. This mental toughness can be illustrated in people who just do not give up, even though all the odds are against them. Recently Ellen Macarthur, the British yachtswoman who finished second in the Vendée Globe race in January 2001 showed remarkable resilience to keep fighting to the end of the race when her yacht encountered all sorts of difficulties along the way. Her story received a lot of media attention perhaps because she was a successful female who had achieved her goals while competing in a male-dominated environment.

She also showed her emotions at times in the documentary footage that was shown after the race. The viewers witnessed her carrying out a repair balanced at the end of the 60-foot mast while at sea and then breaking down in tears afterwards because it had taken so much out of her. But despite showing these emotions, Ellen would bounce back with remarkable resilience and carry on to face the next challenge that nature threw at her and her yacht. It is precisely this ability to endure emotionally testing situations and to carry on time after time that shows true peak performers apart from other people.

This research also supports the earlier work of Daniel Goleman whose book *Working with Emotional Intelligence* outlines exactly this concept. He argues that successful people in business today are likely to have not only a high level of IQ which we know as the measure of cognitive intelligence, but in addition they possess a high level of EQ which he describes as a measure of emotional intelligence. Daniel Goleman carried out a series of studies into competence models drawn from 121 companies worldwide. He found that EQ (the ability to be aware of, and manage one's emotions) mattered twice as much as IQ (having the cognitive ability to solve problems etc.) across all types of jobs.

Kickstart Tip

> ### Hints on motivating yourself for success
>
> - Recognize what you want to achieve ensuring that it is in alignment with your true values and beliefs
> - Create energy and enthusiasm for your goal
> - Take some *action* to try to achieve it
> - Keep reviewing and reflecting on progress, to ensure that you are heading in the direction you want to go
> - Be aware of the messages that you are telling yourself, and how they impact on your goal, e.g. *I am not very good at athletics, because I came last in the race.* (Change the message to *I could be better at athletics, and I will improve my start for the next time*)

Messages that Shape Our Beliefs

The messages we receive in early childhood can impact on our belief about what we are capable of. When I was young I used to love reading adventure books and marvelled at how people like Sir Edmund Hillary or Sir Chay Blyth could achieve such feats as climbing Mount Everest or rowing across the Atlantic. It seemed to a child like me that in order to be a successful adventurer you had to have two qualities – you had to be a man, and you had to have a lot of money. And being a 9-year-old girl I did not qualify for either, so this made me believe that I could not be an adventurer. It may have been a similar message that Ellen Macarthur received when she was trying to start out in the male-dominated world of sailing and because similar beliefs are often held throughout society, being a successful woman in a male-dominated world or vice versa is all the more challenging.

The beliefs that we develop when we are young can shape us for the rest of our lives. Imagine what happens at a school sports day and a child comes in last in the 100-metre race. Her mother or father shouts to her, 'it's okay darling, don't worry we know you are not good at running'. That statement enters the child's head and remains there. It slowly changes to become a statement of fact whereas it should merely have been an observation at that time. Its impact can be dramatic, and as that child grows up, she believes that she is not good at running. She will probably turn down every opportunity she gets to run and say to herself 'I am not a good runner, so I will not take part'.

The parents are oblivious to the effect that their comment has had on their child and how it can affect her in later years.

It is so often that we hear people as adults say that they did not believe they could do something because someone told them that as a child.

Our beliefs are formed at an early age, and can stay with us for life if we choose not to challenge them. The essence of this book is really about how we can challenge our own individual beliefs to kickstart our motivation. If we want to truly find out what we are capable of, we need to look out for and seize opportunities to test ourselves.

I managed to test my capabilities in 1996 when our team successfully trekked 350 miles to the Magnetic North Pole. It was a journey that I had never imagined was possible for me to attempt, let alone be successful.

Encouragement Reaps Rewards

At school I had an average education, just like anyone else, and was never inspired or motivated to really test myself. The only person that did stand out from schooldays was Margot Wells, our physical education teacher and wife of UK Olympic 100-metre champion Allan Wells. Even when we were out running in the rain, or playing hockey in the sun, she would be there shouting at us, encouraging us, and helping us to succeed.

We could all remember so vividly her enthusiastic shouting that was broadcast on TV nationwide, while Allan sped towards the finishing line in Moscow. It was that same enthusiasm and motivation that helped us at school. Margot noticed that I was quite good at longer-distance running especially in the 3-kilometre cross-country events, and asked me if I would like to join the local Edinburgh running club called Edinburgh Southern Harriers.

At that time, I was rather shy and did not feel particularly keen to go along on my own, and only attended when a friend of mine went too. Even when I did go, there was not really anyone who coached us individually and so it did not last. I lost interest and gave up going to training.

However, what did stick in my head was Margot's encouragement. We had an instant role model, a link to an Olympic champion, and someone who *had* achieved success. It is this type of role model that also can play a major part in how young people behave in future years. Of course, it does not only happen when we are young. Role models can inspire us at any time regardless of our age.

The Value of Role Models

David Hemery, the UK Olympic champion in 1968 and world record holder for 400-metre hurdles, undertook a study in 1986 of what makes high achievers successful. The results that were published in his book *Sporting Excellence* showed that one of the common themes was the impact that other role models had on successful sportsmen and women. Time after time, he discovered that they had been inspired when they were young by seeing someone else achieve a level of success and countless successful people today quote others as their inspiration or role models.

Therefore in society today, we can all have a positive influence on those around us by providing good examples of behaviour or stories of success to which they can aspire. Too often, the type of image that young people see is of violence, a lifestyle of greed, and individualism, which is often promoted by the media. You only have to open a newspaper or watch a film these days to see the type of role models that we are providing for the next generation. Margot Wells provided a positive role model for me. Her enthusiasm and encouragement made me believe that I too could run and be good at it. We can all be a role model for someone.

A recent study that was carried out by a UK consultancy business The Change Partnership to analyse what made 'successful' women leaders showed that two thirds of them attended single-sex schools when they were young. These leaders said that because they observed other women performing many different roles successfully it appeared to be the norm and these experiences gave the girls some excellent role models.

The Role of Mentors in Encouraging Motivation

The value of mentors and role models is not to be underestimated. They play such a critical role particularly with those who are lacking in self-esteem and confidence. Mentoring developed from the concept of apprenticeship where a person more experienced in their craft would pass on their knowledge to someone less experienced.

Today, it has developed from that to encompass the idea that the person who is performing the mentoring role does not necessarily need to understand the business of the person being mentored. The relationship is more that of coach and performer, where the coach will use questions and encouragement to help the performer take responsibility for their own development. In this way, the ownership for change rests with the performer and not with the mentor or coach.

Parents traditionally provide a role model for children and what can sometimes happen is that the parents use their own experiences to shape their children's future. For example, if they had an average education and then went immediately into a job, then they may encourage their children to do the same, while it may not be appropriate for them to do so. Parents need to be aware of how influential they are and how their own experiences and values may creep into what they perceive their children can achieve.

When we develop from children to adults, and do join the business world, we also need to have role models and mentors in that environment to help us make our way. Many organizations these days have a mentoring scheme and actively encourage their graduates and new employees to achieve success. The mentor's role is to help the individual to find an appropriate way to develop their career and to find out about all the potential opportunities that they may wish to take. Their next job may not be the next level up within that organization. It could be in a completely different area of business. Although a mentor does not have to be an expert in the area of business that the individual works, it helps for the mentor to have a varied experience in the business world, as they can then offer their knowledge to the individual if required.

Kickstart Tip

Benefits of a mentoring programme

- It gives the mentors a sense of personal satisfaction that they have been able to help other employees to develop
- Individuals can feel that the organization 'cares' about them even if they are not in a job for life
- There are huge benefits particularly in terms of developing one's self-esteem and getting encouragement

Taking Responsibility for Our Own Success

In business today there is no longer a 'job for life' culture and as individuals we need to plan our own future, and not rely on the organization to plan it for us. In this scenario, the role of a mentor or role model becomes even more valuable. We need to consider our transferable skills and the value that we can gain from each job we undertake. This can help us to plan our own career with a clearer focus and not be task-specific within one organization, but think more laterally. For example, a person working at a call-centre for an insurance company would probably have excellent interpersonal skills, be able to summarize effectively and be capable of working under pressure. They would also be able to utilize these skills in many other industry areas.

Recognizing the Company Values

As you move from one organization to another during your career, understanding more about how a company values their people can give you some clues as to how your values may or may not match theirs. You may feel that family-friendly policies are important within a company particularly if you have children. It would therefore be vital to carry out some research to find out if an organization does have any such policies in existence prior to applying for any vacancies that might exist.

Those companies that do value their people will demonstrate this by their actions at all stages of a person's career. From providing outplacement courses prior to retiring to offering extensive training packages, a wealth of benefits and exciting career opportunities to encourage new graduates, this shows that the welfare of their staff is extremely important to them, even if they do accept that individuals may not expect to stay in the company for long. For example, Merrill Lynch expects that most graduates will stay with their company for no more than three to four years, yet they invest a lot of money into their graduate programme to attract the best people into the company.

Some simple questions that you could ask the company before you make a decision to join could be:

- How would you describe the culture of your organization?
- What benefits does the company provide to demonstrate that it values its people?
- What opportunities might exist for me to be creative, empowered, and truly have the chance to make a difference?

● What policies do you have in place to address work/life balance issues?

The answers to those questions may give you a clue about how people are valued within a workplace. But the real test is, if you get the chance, to visit the company and within a few minutes of sitting at the reception it is possible to learn more about an organization than you would do in any company literature. Listen to how the phone is answered, how colleagues talk to one another, how you are treated when you arrive and all these actions will give you more meaningful information about the company culture.

Recently I worked with a large housing organization that stated that 'our people are our greatest asset' in their company values statement. However, it was clear to me that there was a great deal of apathy among their employees. During the day I accompanied one of the senior team to join the queue for the buffet lunch. Ahead of us was a long line of employees eagerly awaiting their meal and I was happy to line up behind them. However, the senior executive hustled me to the front of the line along with himself to cut in front of all the other staff. I was extremely embarrassed at this situation but it demonstrated to me that although their values statement outlined that they valued their people, in reality their behaviour was not congruent. As the saying goes, 'actions speak louder than words' and in this case it certainly showed.

In summary, organizations that *do* take actions to support their values and beliefs are likely to have the following characteristics:

Kickstart Tip

Companies who value their people are likely to:

- Provide real opportunities for people to be empowered and have an element of choice and responsibility within their work
- Encourage and support their employees through a mentoring or coaching programme
- Help their employees to gain a balance between life and work
- Recognize that developing the combination of emotional intelligence and cognitive intelligence within their people should help them to develop into peak performers.

Just as Margot Wells encouraged us at school to believe we were capable of running fast, organizations will need to find the means to encourage their people to achieve their potential too. They would then be tapping into the true capabilities of their most valuable asset – their people. Once organizations have found a way to make this happen, amazing things can occur.

Summary

1. Peak performers possess all three components of *Learned Powerfulness*™ – *Focus, Authenticity, Resilience*.

2. Be aware of how the messages that you received as a child impact on your behaviour.
3. Encouragement from others can reap great rewards.
4. Don't underestimate the value of role models.
5. Mentors have a key role to play in encouraging motivation.
6. Each of us needs to take responsibility for our own success.
7. Ask focused questions to find out if a company lives by its stated values, e.g. what policies do they have to address work/family issues and how effective are they?
8. Organizations that value people are more likely to attract and retain them more effectively.

Chapter 2

Testing Your Capabilities

In this chapter we examine:

- Seizing opportunities
- Risk taking
- Preparation and planning
- Managing change

Very often when I am speaking in large companies, people tell me that they would love to go off for a sabbatical or unpaid leave and take part in a real 'adventure'. It seems that although they are passionate about work, they still want to really test themselves physically and mentally to the limit. Others want to benefit others in some kind of charity work. Ultimately in both cases they can learn about what they are capable of while working with others.

With this need in mind, there are a myriad of organizations that have set themselves up in recent years to provide this opportunity for people. From cycling across Cuba for Cancer Research to spending three months diving while carrying out an environmental study, it is possible to volunteer for all sorts of projects and learn more about your strengths, weaknesses and motivations at the same time.

This chapter illustrates one such adventure that took place in 1988, on an expedition known then as Operation Raleigh. British Gas was a corporate supporter of Operation Raleigh and saw it as an excellent way to develop some of its employees. The experience they could gain from a three-month expedition would ultimately enhance their potential back in the business. Employees could develop their self-confidence, their ability to work under pressure and in teams, an understanding of how to work with limited resources and their own thinking about what they are capable of.

The real essence of a Raleigh Expedition was to develop young people while at the same time providing some real benefit to the local community where it operated. The learning that those who participate in it get from such an experience is almost unmeasurable but certainly for many it 'changed their life'.

The Opportunity

One day, I was reading the features on the notice board at work, when a brightly coloured poster caught my eye. It showed people climbing, and trekking in many different environments, and stated 'Are you aged between 17 and 25 and able to swim 25 metres?' In fact it was an advert for an Operation Raleigh expedition where young people could spend three months in remote parts of the world, carrying out scientific community and adventure projects. Operation Raleigh is a UK-based charity that was set up in 1984 and took *venturers* to remote parts of the world by ship. Venturer is the name given to those who participated in the expeditions. By 1988 the adventures had moved to land-based expeditions in countries such as Alaska, Kenya, Australia and Uganda.

The only information that I had about the expeditions was how they went about selecting their participants. I had heard that they made people hold a tarantula in their hand for a few seconds, and even though the idea frightened me, I also thought it might be fun to go through this strange experience. Fortunately this had only been a publicity stunt and did not actually take place on our selection weekend!

British Gas sponsored only five employees per year to take part in the expeditions, and in an organization of 30 000 employees, competition for places was fierce. The process began with a written application, and if you successfully passed that stage, a rigorous 36-hour selection weekend was the next test. Having decided to apply I approached my manager for approval because if successful, this would mean 3 months away from the office while being paid! He supported my application, and we sent it the organizers.

Two of us from the Scottish Region of the company, myself and John Buchanan, a graduate engineer, were invited to the British Gas selection weekend scheduled to take place in October 1987 on Saddleworth Moor, near Oldham in Lancashire. It was only once I had received the letter of confirmation that the reality of what I was trying to do hit me. We had been given a list of items to take on the weekend, including rucksack, sleeping bag, and walking boots plus a 'hand-made' wooden implement which could be used to eat!

I did not own any of these items, far less know how to make a wooden implement and had to beg and borrow boots and all the other pieces of kit to ensure I was ably equipped for any eventuality. Even the wooden implement fashioned from a branch was a major achievement for me to create. I think having seen films of cavemen catching dinner by using a long spear gave me the wrong idea of what this implement was likely to be used for!

Kickstart Tip

> ## Testing your commitment
>
> - The first challenges that you face will test your commitment to the goal.
> - If a person is not wholeheartedly passionate about what they want to achieve, then they are likely to give up even at this early stage, if the challenges seem too great.

Using Information to Minimize Risk Taking

We arrived at the youth hostel near Saddleworth Moor on the Friday evening, nervous about what might await us. Thirty other hopefuls had travelled from twelve other regions of the UK, and we all talked together, speculating what might await us over the next 36 hours. One girl had already taken part in a selection weekend but had been unsuccessful and therefore slipped us several pieces of useful advance information. She told us about how we would not be able to have any food with us, how we would get wet, and what the selectors were looking for was our ability to work together as a team. I guess these things were already fairly obvious, but it made us feel good to think that we had some advance information about the programme.

Entrepreneurs in business also rely on their network of contacts to get as much information as possible about opportunities before they make a decision. There is a popular misconception that entrepreneurs are high risk-takers, but they actually take calculated risks. They will collect as much information as possible using their network of contacts to minimize any risks or problems. It is always useful to collect as much information as possible before taking any action. However, sometimes in teams people do not bother to ask about the level of knowledge or experience within a group before they start a task, and they then are likely not to use the available resources most effectively.

Enthusiasm is the Key Ingredient

Saturday morning dawned crisply cold and bright, and I nervously stood in-line on the playing fields awaiting instructions. Immediately we had to unpack our rucksacks and I was a little embarrassed at its meagre contents – because as a non-outdoors person, it had only the basics inside. Other people who obviously were seasoned outdoors specialists seemed to have prepared for a month-long expedition, and had all sorts of items spilling out of their rucksacks. I felt rather the poor relation at this stage.

It did not matter a bit, because the organizers immediately had us packing up someone else's rucksack and then running off with rucksacks in tow to undertake a challenging assault course. I had little enough idea of what had been in my rucksack when I had packed it and now I did not have a clue where anything was. Luckily, we did not really need too many items as the weather was kind to us and remained dry but cold.

This fast pace continued throughout the weekend, and we were to be well and truly exhausted by the time Sunday afternoon arrived. This was the first time I had experienced really adventurous outdoor activities, such as rafting and orienteering. It was exhilarating, and I gained in confidence during the weekend adding to our team my limited knowledge of map reading or navigation or just cracking a joke when things got tough. Overall I just tried to be enthusiastic about each new challenge we were set by the assessors.

Kickstart Tip

Gaining confidence

- Review your progress once you have taken your first risk, and it is likely that you will have gained in confidence.
- Even if the risk has been unsuccessful, there will be the opportunity to learn from the experience.

As we had been warned, the selectors from Operation Raleigh were not just looking for our skills in map reading or first aid. Instead, what they were interested in was our ability to get on with one another, how we interacted when the going got tough, and how we helped or hindered one another while undertaking challenging tasks.

One of the tasks we were given was to build a raft out of four wooden planks and four plastic barrels. To help us we had a quantity of rope and within 45 minutes we had to devise a plan, build the raft and transport ourselves plus our equipment across a freezing lake that stretched about 50 metres in diameter.

After a few minutes debating how we would set about this task, we came up with a plan and set to work. Lashing together barrels and planks was not the most familiar activity for me in the world, but with the idea that if we did not construct a sturdy raft we would end up in the freezing water, it helped to focus our minds. Even with all our best efforts we began to run out of time, and consequently as we rushed and all tried to dive on the raft and paddle it across the lake the quality of our construction was obviously lacking and most people ended up in the water. At least we all laughed and had smiles on our faces. That ability to be cheerful in adversity would be useful on many, many occasions for me in later life.

In the workplace, these types of outdoor challenge courses are hugely popular these days to encourage corporate teamwork, communication and leadership skills. The objective is not just to have fun in the outdoors but also to ensure that the teams review their experiences and are able to understand how the learning applies back in their work environment. It also provides a shared experience of hardship that the employees can refer to back in work that can help to break down barriers between departments and to foster better social relationships.

It is perhaps for this reason that companies use events like Raleigh expeditions to develop their staff, because if they can survive and work together in arduous environments, then they are at least more likely to succeed in the workplace.

Thirty-six hours later and a whole lot smellier we emerged from the weekend in the knowledge that both John and I had been selected as two of the five successful candidates. This was the first time that any people from the Scottish region of British

Gas had been sponsored for an Operation Raleigh expedition, and consequently all the staff became enthusiastic too and willing to help us fund-raise for the expedition. But the challenges had only just begun. Not only was enthusiasm the key ingredient that the organizers had been looking for but also our success had generated a similar level of energy within the company.

Kickstart Tip

Enthusiasm is infectious and rubs off on other people.

Building on Success

Operation Raleigh's ethos was to provide four challenges:

1. To get through the selection weekend
2. To raise the funds required
3. To undertake the expedition
4. To put something back into the local community.

The fourth challenge provided a tangible benefit for local people in the UK too because each *venturer* was encouraged to undertake some type of community project to continue supporting their local area at the end of the expedition. This challenge was trying to build on the energy and enthusiasm that the *venturer* would probably have at the end of the expedition and Operation Raleigh's goal was to help focus that energy in a constructive manner.

Kickstart Tip

> ### *Maintaining motivation*
>
> Before you have completed your goal, it is critical to at least start thinking about the next goal to maintain motivation and focus.

John and I now both had to undertake the second challenge – that of raising £1500. Although British Gas was sponsoring us by paying the expedition costs, the challenge for all venturers is to raise a sum of money. The funds we raised would then help pay for others who were from disadvantaged backgrounds to go on the Raleigh expedition too.

The goal of raising such a large sum of money now seemed much more achievable as John and I had gained a level of confidence. Once a person has taken that step into the unknown and it has been relatively successful, we learn from it and can gain confidence to face the next challenge. The first step is always the toughest, and many people never proceed past that trying to take that action.

Using Passion to Make Fund-raising Easier

Anyone who has ever had to raise money for a cause will know that it is never easy. There are so many competing worthy causes these days that you need to have a pretty strong case as to why people should help you. What really helps in this situation is to have a little passion. If you truly believe in, and are passionate about, the cause that you are raising money for, then it is certainly easier to fund-raise. I am sure that we have all encountered times in our lives when someone has invited you to help their cause. People do not have to be pushy or forceful, but yet one can tell if they are really passionate about their cause. Their eyes light up as they speak, and their facial expressions show how they really feel about the cause. These non-verbal signals are just as alluring as the spoken word.

Kickstart Tip

Demonstrating passion

- Passionate people use not only words to convey their message.
- They also use non-verbal communications such as smiling, hand movements, and their bodies. For example, some nationalities such as Italians generally communicate in this manner.
- This means that they are communicating on an intellectual and an emotional level at the same time.

What helped both John and I was the fact that this was a first for the Scottish Region within British Gas. That meant we could gain maximum publicity within the company in Scotland and that other employees were not jaded by past participants' attempts at fund-raising. We set about our task of raising £3000 in total, and decided to organize several joint events, where we could split the proceeds.

Operation Raleigh provided lots of help and ideas on how to go about raising the money. One day I was speaking to another employee who had participated from another Region and I learnt from her that she had organized a plastic duck race, where she had 1000 plastic ducks and floated them in a race down a stream in her village. The person having bought the duck that reached the finishing line first would win a prize.

I decided that this could be a novel way of raising money and asked her if I could borrow the plastic ducks. So the idea was developed to have a plastic duck race and get them to float a few metres down the Water of Leith in Edinburgh. They were all numbered and so we decided to sell tickets as a type of lottery and get local businesses to donate prizes. It seemed to be a unique method at the time, and consequently people both inside British Gas and outside the company bought tickets. The money came pouring in and eventually the whole event raised almost half of the amount required. The biggest headache was trying to catch 1000 plastic ducks after they had crossed the finishing line and then ensuring that they were all present and correct. It was an amusing sight later that evening when all the ducks were lined up in numerical order on my living room carpet!

It was during this period that I began to feel apprehensive about the expedition for the first time. Thoughts began to go through my head like – 'what if I don't raise all the money?' or 'what if I can't cope on the expedition?' Until now the whole process had been a bit of a whirlwind, and I had suddenly to take stock of what this would *actually* mean in terms of living out in the wilds for three months of my life.

Sometimes we can get so caught up in what we are doing, whether it's work, or home life, that we forget to sit down and really think about what is happening. Of course, if our subconscious has already done that, then that can be precisely the reason why we keep busy, because we don't want to face reality. Looking back I now understand that if we really do want to succeed in what we are doing, we need to address our fears and not let them build up and overcome us.

Overcoming Fear

One way to overcome our fears is to write them down, or to actually articulate them. Expressing what our fears are is often the first step towards overcoming them. If you can take a long hard look at what you are frightened of it is almost as if you are putting them on show and then once you can see them you can deal with them. You might consider questions such as:

- What are the things I fear about this issue?
- What is the thing that I fear most?
- What is the reason for that?
- What might be the worst possible outcome?
- What could I do if that situation arose?
- What opportunities might that situation bring?
- What can I do to overcome these fears?

Another method to use is to find a mentor or a coach with whom you can work. They can help you by merely asking questions and provoking thought – helping you to address what stops you moving forward. It is only by becoming aware and then taking the personal responsibility to do something about it that change takes place.

People also find that inertia can be overpowering and they end up being frightened to do anything for fear of it being the wrong route to choose. Having spoken to many people about this issue, I would suggest that one option is to be able to identify an action that you do feel good about taking. It could be as simple as deciding to make a phone call, or to sit down and think about your issue, but the important point is that you are taking action. Very often it will not matter really what that action is, but the fact that you are *doing* something helps. It has taken you to a new place, and a new perspective.

Kickstart Tip

> ### Avoiding inertia
> - Identify just one action that you feel good about taking.
> - The more you avoid it, the more difficult it gets to take any action.

The former motor racing driver John Whitmore in his best-selling book, *Coaching for Performance*, developed a model for coaching called the GROW model. This has four elements:

> **G** oal –   What do you want to achieve?
> **R** eality –   What is happening now?
> **O** ptions – What could you do?
> **W** ill –   What will you do?

By the coach asking appropriate questions of the individual at each stage, the person can raise their own awareness of what will help them to move forward to achieve their goal. They then need to generate responsibility to take action.

Often it can feel daunting to embark on a new challenge or make a change in your life, but if you have thought through all the potential problems in advance then it can help in the process of being committed to any actions. Eventually what really helped me was to remind myself why I was doing this and therefore why it was so vital to raise the money.

Preparation and Planning

Preparation and planning are keys to success of any project and it is just the same in business. You need to prepare and think ahead to ensure that you have considered all the potential problems, how you can overcome them, and also in this case, how I would be able to survive in this new type of environment for a prolonged period of time.

Even though I did not know if I would survive without washing for days, or eating decent food, or living in a tent, I *did* know that I was flexible enough to just get on with whatever life threw at me. It is this resilience and determination that I guess the organizers had been looking for on the selection weekend.

Our expedition began in September 1988, ten months after being selected. I had chosen Kenya as my destination and 120 of us arrived from all over the world to begin this expedition that would literally change my life.

A house in the suburbs of Nairobi served as the field base for the expedition and it was here that we gathered with the leaders to be told what we would be doing. An Operation Raleigh expedition is three months long as described earlier and is divided up into three segments each lasting three weeks during which the venturers would undertake scientific, community and adventure projects. Each of these 'phases', as they were known, would mean working with a new team, thus providing plenty of opportunity for meeting new people and experiencing a variety of locations in the country. The remaining time was used in the changeover periods from one project to another and the training phase to become acclimatized with living and working in the country.

The young people came from all over the world – the UK, the USA, Australia, New Zealand, as well as local venturers from Kenya itself. It was a balanced mix of men and women, from all sorts of backgrounds: corporate venturers like myself who had been sponsored by companies, people who perhaps were unemployed or homeless and who had been able to participate due to the funding that we had raised prior to the expedition, and others who had just applied individually.

Imagine what the atmosphere was like when 120 young people came together who had all had to raise a substantial amount of money just to get to this stage of the expedition. Everyone seemed to have already such an incredible level of commitment to the cause that it must have been fairly frightening for the volunteer staff. They would have to help ensure that we all achieved what we wanted to from such an experience. The staff would also have to avoid getting downhearted or demotivated due to the frequent changes in plan because of the nature of the work that we were doing. It was an amazing experience.

Our projects were located all over Kenya. Our community project was in the Northern Frontier District in a small remote village called Opiroi, a day's walk from Maralal, one of the stopping points for tourists journeying up to Lake Turkana.

There was no medical dispensary for the local people, and so our task was to begin the foundations of a simple building that would serve this purpose.

Flexibility is Key to Survival

As we expected the expedition did not go according to plan. This is often the situation in the business world too. A team can spend months creating a new computer system or developing a new product only to find that the finished item hardly resembles the original plan due to many changes made along the way. In this regard, individuals need be flexible because the business environment in particular changes so quickly that to survive these days you need to have one eye on what you are developing and the other on what the competition is doing. In the IT market in particular, radical changes in technology are now happening in a matter of months whereas new technology used to take years to develop. This impacts on speed of design and production and means that rather than producing complicated designs that are difficult to change, technology is moving towards more simple but flexible designs that can accommodate changes more easily, e.g. in mobile phone design.

Similarly, on an expedition, problems encountered have to be solved in imaginative ways by using simple but flexible designs. While trying to lay the foundations for the dispensary, it became clear that the aggregate for the concrete was not likely to arrive for several weeks. What would you do in this situation?

We decided to collect it ourselves. This meant that we spent days on our hands and knees; picking up small stones all of a similar size so that we could use this as aggregate instead. In this way we were still able to achieve our goal but not perhaps in the manner we had first imagined!

Companies can be successful if they maintain flexibility and respond to changing customer needs. A good example would be Federal Express, the courier company that continually introduces new improvements in service to help their customers. Another is General Electric, whose success was reported by the Anglo-Norwegian consultancy The Performance Group as being built on continual breakthroughs in every area of their business.

Kickstart Tip

> ### Flexibility
>
> Ensure that you are mentally prepared to make changes to your plan. It is highly likely that the results will not be achieved as expected. Ongoing flexibility is key to survival.

In business unfortunately the only time that organizations regularly face tough challenges are when their backs are against the wall and they are literally trying to survive. When organizations are put into that position, they go back to basics – they focus on the core business and try to ensure that it thrives. This is the strategy that several of the large UK retail companies seem to be using following the announcement that US retail giant Wal-Mart will be coming to the UK. Wal-Mart's strategy to pile 'em high, sell 'em cheap drives out smaller businesses from wherever they go. Their main competitors have to decide how they will face this challenge. It means keeping their eye on the ball and ensuring that they can provide their core product well enough and at a low enough price to keep their customers. Only time will tell if their strategy in the UK is successful.

More generally, the advent of the web and dot.com companies has threatened the status quo of many traditional bricks and mortar companies who have had to rethink their marketing strategies in the light of this new situation. However, market research has shown that customers still recognize and trust well-known brands on the web more than some of the newer names that have appeared and this does give traditional companies some advantage if they then choose to have an online presence.

Team Issues

When our first group was announced on the Raleigh expedition there were ten of us in the team, a Kenyan, a New Zealander, an Australian, an American and several Brits. One man in the team, Paul, was deaf so that was an additional challenge that we all had to overcome. We decided together to learn the basics of sign language and try to speak for an hour or so every day only using these signs. This idea was great in theory but did not always work in practice. When the stresses and strains of living in a remote Kenyan community got to people, it seemed that they were less able to continue the commitment of speaking in that way – even if it was just for an hour! However, Paul was often able to pick up the meaning of what was happening and it was a situation that we all just had to learn to handle.

In business, we can find ourselves operating in a similar manner sometimes. There could be a person in the department or team who appears to be less able to work at the same level as others and it can lead to a source of frustration. If these types of issues are not dealt with straightaway, then they can lead to even greater problems later when the frustration and resentment builds up.

It takes courage to address these types of issues at times, and in our situation out in Kenya, we just had to learn to get on with the task while recognizing that Paul was just as much a valued member of our team as any other person. We had to try to take his needs into account. However, the selfishness in others can raise its head when the going gets tough and they revert back to ensuring that only their survival is paramount.

Kickstart Tip

Valuing diversity

An effective team is one that recognizes and values the diversity of qualities that are found within each individual whether they are related to race, religion, disability or gender.

On our expedition specialist roles were not allocated to any particular people, but more beneficially a 'day leader' kind of system was encouraged that gave each person in the group an opportunity to experience the role of leader for at least one day. At the end of their session a brief review would follow where the others could provide feedback on how well they thought the leader performed and how they could improve for the next time. This fairly informal approach to helping venturers develop worked extremely well and helped each one of us in the team to learn from the experiences that were taking place.

Within a few days, we had all begun to get used to working together. A system for living and working together had been slowly developing, where we as a team agreed how we would operate rather than being directed by the Raleigh staff.

We decided to work from 7 am until 2 or 3 pm depending on how hot it was and then have a sleep. We repeated this for six days and then always took a Sunday off to have a break. The role of the Raleigh staff member is really to facilitate our team working and ensure that we achieve the aim of the project. Ideally this is what could happen in an organization where the manager can facilitate and coach the team to achieving high levels of performance.

Kickstart Tip ✗

Enhancing team performance

Encouraging people to set their own goals, rotating roles within the team to develop flexibility and reviewing performance together regularly can enhance team performance.

During our first project only two people in the team had experience of any type of building work, but this did not matter. It was enthusiasm and determination that helped us all to achieve our goal. The volunteer member of staff provided the technical expertise, and the rest of us just got on with the job of digging and collecting stones.

This was the first time I had ever been involved in any type of building project, and although at times it was hard work, it was a great learning experience. I was committed to playing my part, having spent nine months raising money to get here, and it was (or so I thought at the time) a once in a lifetime experience. We all wanted to make a difference to the local community and this project really was a chance for us to do that.

Many companies these days also have a social responsibility locally and globally and many help to provide opportunities for their employees to volunteer or take part in activities or work with local charities. This not only helps the company to have a positive image locally, but also helps the employees who gain a sense of personal satisfaction.

The UK company The Body Shop uses Third World villages to supply many of the natural ingredients they use in their products, which they see as a form of 'trade, not aid'. Other charities such as Oxfam sell items in their stores that are produced by local labour in Third World countries and they promote fair trade issues by selling coffee purchased directly from the growers, thus ensuring that a fair price is paid to those who actually produce the coffee in the country itself. Even the huge oil companies such as Shell and BP have an environmental responsibility globally not to pursue their own interests to the detriment of the local population or environment.

Stepping Out of Our Comfort Zone

When any of us try a new activity, or seek to change our behaviour, we are stepping into unknown territory, and moving out of our comfort zone. This zone is the world that we exist in where everything is comfortable and we feel happy and confident to cope with any challenges or new experiences that we might face. There can be several reasons why we move out of it – e.g. we may wish to seek a new opportunity, or to get away from danger or a threat, or to discover the unknown. Whatever the motivation, once we step out of our comfort zone there are endless opportunities to expand learning and improve performance.

Kickstart Tip

> ### Stepping out of the comfort zone
>
> Learning takes place more quickly and easily if the individual who is stepping outside their zone of comfort has some support.

But we may not feel comfortable in trying to expand this zone of comfort without some support. That's where the role of a coach or supportive friend or leader can be extremely beneficial. They can work with you to find out what you need to feel comfortable in this new environment, and help you find a way to get it. For example, when each of us had the opportunity to take on the role of day leader during the expedition, it was a new experience for many of us. If we had felt that we were going to have no support, then perhaps that threat would appear too great and the person would choose to remain in their comfort zone and not try. We had the benefit of working with volunteer staff that understood that we would all have different comfort zones and they would consequently have to provide different levels of support for each of us. That way, they encouraged venturers to really stretch themselves and then have the opportunity for feedback and review at the end of the day.

Managing a Changing Environment

After four weeks of working on one project site, we moved onto another site and the groups changed. It was a traumatic experience because during those four weeks we had built up some close working relationships with the other venturers. Now it was about to change. It is ironic that even in a short period of four weeks I had found some sort of security and safe environment even within the constantly changing environment in which we were operating. People at the end of the day need to find some level of safety and security even in chaos.

It was now onto our adventure phase that consisted of a camel trek to climb Matthews Peak. This mountain, one of the highest in the Northern Frontier District at 2375 metres, is shrouded in bush and trees, making it extremely difficult to access. Our 60-mile journey to get to the mountain was to take eight days across dry open landscapes where temperatures would reach 35°C and higher. By midday any form of exercise became virtually impossible. Our team leader had arranged for us to obtain twelve camels that came with three camel handlers. These beasts were not to be used for us to ride on, but to carry all the water, food and equipment that would be required for this adventure.

Having never worked with camels before, we all had a steep learning curve. They all seemed to have individual personalities, and some spat or bit more than others, which we had to learn quickly! Every morning the camel handlers would show us how to load up the large sacks with equipment. These had to be balanced equally on each side of the camel. The sacks were attached to their saddles and although the camels were hobbled (had their legs tied together) it was a great challenge to try to load the saddles onto them without incurring the green spit from a camel on our clothes. Those of us who were not quick enough to move out of the way would live to regret it, as camel spit is not the most pleasant smelling thing in the world and has a tendency to linger!

Once the saddle with all its equipment was loaded then the camels would be unhobbled and tied nose to tail in three lines. We would walk alongside them or lead the front one. Even trying to do this was fraught with problems, particularly if we were heading through an area with lots of trees or obstacles. The camels had minds of their own and would decide that the route that the lead camel took was not the best one. Consequently the second or third camel would choose a different one and immediately the lead camel would let out a horrendous squeal as it felt its tail being dragged in a different direction! The second camel would continue to walk and the noise would get louder. When we tried to push the camel with a stick the correct way, we risked being spat on so all in all we had to keep our wits about us. By the time we had spent a week with these creatures we had developed a bond with them, and almost knew their individual personalities as well as we knew the people we were trekking with.

Kickstart Tip

Getting to know your team

When you have to work in a team environment, (even if it's with animals), the quicker you get to know what motivates each individual, the quicker you will be able to adapt your behaviour to get the best from each person (or animal)!

The major benefit was that we were able to walk along each day, with just small day sacks containing water, food and our cameras that made the journey in the searing heat a little more bearable. Every day we got up at around 6 am and were able to leave sometimes before 7 am. This meant that the majority of our trekking was done before the hottest part of the day. It was heavenly to be able to find a shady spot to lie under in the afternoon, as the sun beat down from the sky and we had covered another few miles towards Matthews Peak. Once we reached the base of the mountain, we left the camels with their handlers and proceeded ourselves on foot with a local guide. It took three days of fighting through dense undergrowth and climbing up sheer slopes to reach the summit. What a sense of achievement we all felt to have conquered a mountain in such a remote area.

Feeling Invincible

Our third phase was the scientific project that was based at a camp near Lake Baringo, one of the Rift Valley lakes. There were several science projects operating from this camp with scientists from the UK spending months studying a variety of life from the fish population in the lake itself to the grasshoppers that lived around it.

Each scientist used the venturers to help them with their research and this meant we had a great deal of variety during the four weeks. It was a beautiful part of Kenya, rich in wildlife and dramatic scenery. In the evening, the noise of hippos emanated from the lakeshore and during the day, crocodiles were to be seen lazing on the shores of the river. We took plenty of opportunities to see as much of the wildlife that Kenya has to offer as possible, even risking our lives to drive up the river early in the morning in an inflatable boat to see the crocodiles while they were still half-asleep!

Although I was now in yet another new team with different people it did not take long for us all to get to know one another and to begin to work together effectively. I think that by this stage we just got on with what needed to be done almost in an unspoken agreement to work together as we all instinctively fitted into the routine of camp life.

The expedition eventually drew to a close and we were able to reflect on what had taken place during the last three months. Many of us had developed lifelong friendships with others from all over the world and we all felt that we had contributed something to the local Kenyan community in one way or another.

Although there had been many times when I had felt exhausted or not able to go on somehow, the other people I had been with had been able to provide support and encouragement. Similarly, when we had undertaken tasks that had been alien to most of us prior to the expedition such as plastering a wall, or lighting a fire out in the bush, we had gained a feeling of accomplishment and of being able to survive in all situations.

I will never forget the atmosphere back in base camp as we all returned at the end of our third project full of tales of what we had done. With 120 people eagerly recounting stories together, the energy and vitality was electric. It is that atmosphere that cannot be easily re-created or described to those sponsors who had helped the venturers to get there in the first place.

I felt that now I was capable of achieving anything. If it was possible to survive for three months in harsh conditions, and make a positive difference to people's lives, then what else was possible? I desperately wanted to be out using these newfound talents that I had discovered and it was going to be interesting to see what would happen as soon as I arrived back down to earth with a bump in British Gas. Time would tell if this experience had been beneficial.

Summary

1. Opportunities are all around. The ability is to know when to seize them.
2. Collect as much information as you can in order to minimize risk taking.
3. Enthusiasm is infectious. It is one of the key ingredients for success.
4. Once you have taken the first risk, the next one never seems so hard.
5. Be passionate about what you are trying to achieve. People then know you are genuine and it demonstrates your belief in the goal.
6. Remind yourself why you are taking that risk, it can help to minimize the fear.
7. Effective preparation and planning is critical. Failing to plan is planning to fail.
8. In these turbulent days of change, flexibility is the key to survival.

9. A team that is performing well has a common goal, understands and accepts each others' strengths and weaknesses and recognizes individual contributions.
10. People only step out their comfort zone when they feel 'safe' to do so.
11. The only stable thing in a world of change should be your mental approach to managing it.
12. The feeling of invincibility can be created through providing the means for people to release more of their potential in a safe environment.

Chapter 3

Building on Success

In this chapter we examine:

- Facing fears
- Values and beliefs
- Harnessing motivation

Returning from any life-changing experience to the normality of a 9–5 job can feel like a complete letdown. If you have experienced major highs and lows in a short time period, then going back to the office can appear to be mundane and boring. This transition period can hit many people. Whether it's returning to work after a long holiday, a training course or an expedition, people do not like taking a step backwards.

This integration of a different experience into the 'normal' way of life is a process that organizations and individuals need to be aware of and to tackle in an appropriate manner.

Millions of pounds are spent annually in the UK on training, but how much time and effort is spent considering this integration stage? Yet this is the most critical stage in the entire learning process I would argue. If it is not handled well, then it can have a negative effect on the entire experience.

What Happens to Integrate Learning?

An individual undertakes a new experience, and that takes a place within their consciousness. If it has been a pleasurable new experience, the individual wants to continue that feeling when they return to 'normal'. If they have learnt a new skill, they want to keep practising it or if they changed their behaviour, they want to continue behaving that way.

Yet the normal environment that they find themselves in is often not able to adapt to that change. In the workplace colleagues may not be able to adapt to that person's new behaviour or they may not be happy that they have learnt a new skill. It will mean change not only for the individual but also for their colleagues, as they have to also adapt their behaviour.

Do we like change? I believe that people do thrive on change. Yet the difference is that if we choose it ourselves we are more likely to be committed to it, rather than it being 'done to us'.

For example, we like to go on holiday, move house or buy a car regularly yet we fear change at work if we are not in control of it. So for me the secret is to introduce a level of choice into change at work.

Returning from a new experience into the workplace, we can choose to remain as we were before, or we can consciously choose to adapt. Sometimes this can be difficult especially if there is no support from your colleagues or manager.

When I returned to British Gas in December 1988, I knew from that day I was not destined to be an accountant or work within finance. The expedition had somehow changed my life, and I had a gut feeling that I needed to be working to help other people learn or change their lives in some way. The enjoyment of making correct calculations and forecasting cash income and outgoings while having little interaction with people was not going to make such a satisfying job now.

Harnessing Motivation to Benefit Both the Individual and the Company

It was lucky that we had a very forward-thinking Employee Development Manager, who recognized the value of the investment that British Gas had made and wanted to ensure that neither John nor I would become disillusioned and leave. He listened carefully as we both enthused about our experiences on the expedition. Then he said 'your old job is going to seem mundane now'. How right he was! I wanted a challenge, something different that would encourage me to maintain this level of motivation and commitment. We discussed what I would really like to do and I wanted to move into training. British Gas had a rather grand training department in an old Georgian manor house, and everyone was envious of those who worked there in the salubrious surroundings.

I guess the manager was a little unsure of my motives – whether I just wanted a cushy place to work, or really whether I was cut out to be a trainer. Luckily British Gas was a large enough organization where one could move from one department to another without too much difficulty and so he arranged for me to join the department on a six-month trial. He also said that if this was going to work he would need me to commit to staying at least two years in the job. What a shrewd move. This gave me the chance to really prove what I could do but at the same time I had to add some commitment to the deal. We shook on it, and a few weeks later I started working in the manor house.

Kickstart Tip

> ### Assessing your personal qualities
>
> Assess your key qualities and how they could be best used within the environment where you work. Get a second opinion from someone that you trust to check out if your perceptions are correct. Write down the list of qualities and refer to them, particularly when you are not feeling so positive.

Obviously in many companies this would not be possible. What is important to consider is what you can offer a company as an individual that would make them want to take a risk and offer you something in which you have no track record. Research has shown that men typically will apply for jobs when they are only currently capable of doing 25 per cent of the advertised job whereas women tend to make sure they feel confident in all areas before applying. This needs to be considered by both organizations in terms of the methods they choose to recruit people and also by individuals when they are considering an application for a post. What is stopping women in particular believing that they are capable of being successful?

Helping Others to Help Yourself

Now that I had grabbed the opportunity to work in an area of the business that I was passionate about, there were new challenges to face. It was a great chance to help other people to develop, which is what attracted me to the job in the first place. During the years that I worked there, there were many occasions to learn more about how people develop, what motivates people, and how to help them learn. The years I spent working in the training department were going to be the building blocks for later years, although I was not aware of it at the time.

For those who do not have a choice about moving to another job, there are other approaches they can take. Choices and opportunities can be created within one's own mind to look for ways to make improvements.

Maybe there are no opportunities to develop your skills or change your behaviour within your workplace, but there are many opportunities that can be taken outside work to develop yourself. Look for skills you can develop at an evening class, or take up a new sport or hobby. These types of activities can provide new challenges too.

Of course, Operation Raleigh recognized that their venturers need another focus on return from their expeditions and that is why the fourth challenge existed. This was to give something back to the local community that had helped to enable you to take part in the expedition in the first place.

As there were also many other Scottish young people who had been on other Raleigh expeditions and were in the same situation it made sense to work together. One of these people had an idea. He, along with some friends, had found an old bothy, which is a traditional Scottish stone-built cottage, in a remote glen near Glencoe in the north-west of Scotland. It was 20 minutes' walk from the nearest road, and was only accessible by foot across a bog, or over the River Etive if it was not too fast flowing. This bothy was in a state of disrepair and had not been lived in for several years.

He had a vision that this bothy could become the focus for former Raleigh venturers to become involved in helping the local community. He dreamed that he and others like him could arrange to run weekend courses there, almost like mini-expeditions, where the young people could renovate the building and also learn about the outdoor environment and take part in adventurous activities. The participants could come from disadvantaged backgrounds, perhaps they would be unemployed or from inner-city areas and who had never been given the chance to experience wide-open spaces and working together to achieve a positive aim.

His infectious enthusiasm rubbed off on those of us who had just returned from the expedition and were also keen to re-create that expedition experience in our own country. And so in early 1989, I joined several others and we drove up to the bothy to undertake some renovation work.

The location of the bothy was truly inspirational. It was based at the foot of Ben Starav, a 3000-foot mountain rising straight from sea level at Loch Etive. The view across the landscape was towards the twin peaks of Buchaille Etive Mhor and Buchaille Etive Beag, which means *Great Shepherd of the Glen* and *Little Shepherd of the Glen*. With no traffic and few people apart from the occasional hill walker passing, it was remarkably quiet and peaceful.

For several months keen volunteers travelled from different parts of Scotland to the bothy to carry out renovation work. The place began to take shape with a new roof-space area created for sleeping, and improved cooking and eating areas within the main room. There was even an outside toilet that was repaired and became fully functional!

This enthusiastic young man also wanted to form the group into a charity because he felt it would be easier to find funding to pay for those young people to attend the weekend courses that he had in mind. And all this started from an idea.

The true entrepreneur has ideas all the time. They can come from different sources. For example, Tom Hunter was an unemployed gradate in Ayrshire, Scotland. He liked to wear training shoes and found that no local shop had a good selection. He noticed that there was a growing demand for training shoes and decided to do something about it. He borrowed money to rent space for a retail outlet and within 10 years had 45 shops with annual sales of £36 million. Another example was Karan Bilimoria, who set up Cobra Beer and became the largest bottler of Indian beer in the UK after noticing that Indian restaurants were becoming popular in Britain.

Kickstart Tip

> ### *Success can come from the smallest idea*
>
> You may think that your idea is ridiculous, yet many successful ventures have begun as a result of a chance conversation, or spotting a gap in the market. Ask yourself what are likely chances of success if you go for it and also what is likely to happen if you don't do it.

In our case Venture Scotland was born. Initially it was just a bunch of committed people who put in lots of volunteer time and effort to organize weekend courses for 12 young people. But it quickly became apparent that there would need to be some form of paid coordinator who would be responsible for fund-raising and finding the right type of participants.

A coordinator was then taken on to fund-raise for the charity. He had to fundraise his own salary plus organize and try to direct the enthusiasm of all these former venturers. There was a lot of work to do, to find these potential participants and to organize a programme that would enable them to benefit from the experience as well as attract funding from trusts and companies who were interested in supporting this charity.

The ingredient that was vital to the organization's success existed in large quantities – that of commitment and passion from those who became part of Venture Scotland. Newcomers commented that they were immediately welcomed into the group and felt that the motivation and commitment from those who were involved rubbed off on them too. Many of my good friends are people that I met through Venture Scotland and they all possess common qualities of open-mindedness and enthusiasm, they have a passion for living and would be willing to help at a moment's notice if there was an emergency. They are the sort of people that you could meet on their doorstep after not being in touch for several years and they would give you a warm welcome and a bed for the night.

Since those humble beginnings, Venture Scotland has since gone from strength to strength. Hundreds of young people have now attended the weekend courses as participants and for many of them it has given them a new level of confidence or opened their eyes to opportunities to become involved in ways of life other than crime or drug-taking. Many volunteer staff had enjoyed the chance to continue on from their Raleigh experiences and achieve that fourth challenge in their own community.

I began to get increasingly involved in working as a volunteer with Venture Scotland. Not only did it re-create some of those adventurous situations that we had experienced on the Raleigh expedition, but it also gave me new challenges. Before I knew it I was Treasurer and then went on the following year to be Chairman, while also leading and helping on many of the courses that we ran at the bothy.

It is now over 12 years since Venture Scotland was established and it is one of the most respected charities in Scotland in its field of expertise. The weekend courses are still run by volunteers and it provides a unique experience for many young people and contributes significantly to their development. And all this began when one person had a clear vision, lots of passion and was willing to take some action to make it happen.

Many companies these days have teamed up with community groups or local charities to enable their staff to volunteer or be involved in some way with their particular cause. Not only does this help the company's image in the local community, it meets that need within people to find something more meaningful than just their 9–5 job, that will help others who perhaps are less fortunate than themselves. We can gain so much personally by giving of our time and energy and therefore it can be a win–win all round for both individuals and charities.

Yet if this passion or motivation within people is not fulfilled within the workplace or in their leisure time, it will begin to eat away within them and can leave them feeling unsatisfied with life. Very often it can eventually lead to the breakdown of relationships as one partner is looking to 'find' him- or herself and the other is reluctant to encourage them, possibly for their own selfish reasons.

I began to experience this after 11 years within British Gas. I was still looking for more adventure, had not found the solution within my job, and was becoming increasingly unsatisfied. It was now time to get out and see what the rest of the big bad world had in store for me.

Kickstart Tip

Integrated and continued learning

As people we never stop learning. Take time to consider what you have learnt over the past year and think about what you would like to learn and how you can achieve it. Failure to satisfy the need to learn or test your capabilities can lead to frustration.

Using Intuition in Decision Making

Once you become aware of wanting to look for something more, then the subconscious can take over and I suddenly realized that I had more than just a passing interest in the job advertisements in the newspaper.

One day while I was reading the *Daily Telegraph*, I noticed a small advert that read '*Opportunities for people not afraid of hard work in a rapidly changing environment*'. Further reading explained that it was a one-year job in the former Yugoslavia working with the United Nations. The post was for a Quality Assurance Officer who would be responsible for helping to improve the efficiency of the civilian operation of the UN mission.

War had broken out in 1992 between the Croats, Serbs and Muslims who had all been held in check during the Tito years. Once he died, trouble began to erupt among the different nations that had all once been part of Yugoslavia. The United Nations had established a peacekeeping mission known as UNPROFOR (United Nations Protection Force) and by early 1994 the numbers of civilian staff working in all areas of the former Yugoslavia numbered 3000 people. Their role was to support the 30 000 troops that came from all over the world. Since the numbers of civilian staff had increased from 300 to 3000 in the space of 18 months, there was basically chaos. Few people knew what the correct United Nations procedures were, and although they were trying their best, there were massive discrepancies between areas of operation. Some people worked efficiently, and others not. Consequently the UN, through its recruitment contractors, advertised for a person to work and help to try to improve this situation.

Latterly I had been working to introduce the concept of continuous improvement and Total Quality within British Gas and so this type of job was just up my street.

I sent off my resumé without that much thought and, amazingly, I had a call a few days later to say that I was on the short list for approval. They would be able to tell me within a week if I had been accepted with a proposed start date four weeks later.

Suddenly, it was time to really think about this life change. I had never seriously considered when I sent in my resumé that it would lead to an offer less than three weeks later. Feeling unsure about what to do I went to speak to my manager. He wisely commented that although the company valued my role, he recognized that eventually there may be other opportunities that I could seize.

This was a courageous step by him because often managers can be loath to allow staff to move on, because they selfishly don't want things to change. Whether he was right and whether this was the right opportunity was down to me to decide.

It's at a time like that when you have to make a major decision that sometimes the best thing to go on is gut-feel. We all too often let the logical part of our brain do the talking and we weigh up the pros and cons without really asking ourselves if we *feel intuitively* that it's the right decision to make.

Kickstart Tip	**Intuitive thinking**
	• Ask yourself what happened to you the last time you listened to your intuitive thoughts.
	• Use this additional ability that you have to assist in making tough decisions.

In this instance, it came down to gut-feel. My friends and family all thought it was a ridiculous idea – why would anyone want to give up a good job, pension scheme, company car, comfortable lifestyle, etc. to embark on a one-year contract with no prospects and in a war zone? Having worked in the company since I was 16, it was all I had ever known and it was extremely frightening to think that I was about to throw all that away and step out into the big bad world. However, I think that if I had stayed any longer the problem would have only become worse and the fears to overcome would just have been greater. Once the decision had been made to leave British Gas I had a great sense of relief, but also there was a nagging sense of fear. This was going to be a major change in my life and it was all going to happen in less than a month, and there was no going back.

Effects of Fear on Behaviour

Fear of change makes people behave very strangely at times in business. Take this example. There was a small office where ten staff worked. One day the boss announced that they would be getting an upgrade to their computer system. This would mean a quicker and more efficient system, but would require some training for everyone.

Several of the staff were really enthusiastic and eagerly awaited the day that the new system would be installed. They had hardly let the computer engineer plug in the machine, when they grabbed the mouse and were immediately keen to find out how much better the software was than what they had before.

Over in the corner, three staff sat with their arms folded defiantly. They immediately complained 'no-one told us it was coming today, how is it going to make our jobs easier, and when do they think we are going to find time to do the training? What a nuisance.' Why were they behaving like that? Of course, it was fear of change and fear of the unknown. Both ways of behaving have their strengths and weaknesses.

Kickstart Tip

Effects of fear on behaviour

- Those who embrace change and ignore past efficiencies and successes are likely to fail when they empty the 'baby out with the bathwater'.
- Those who fear change are not always open to new ways of doing things.
- Become aware of how you behave in fearful situations and then you will be in a better position to decide if you want to modify that behaviour.

What can help in this type of situation is to understand why the change is taking place. Once people understand this then they are in a position to make a choice. They can choose how they will react to the situation. It's either like it and learn how the new system works, or choose to look elsewhere for employment. There are always choices, even though the person having to choose may not like the options.

Suddenly I went from teaching people about managing change, to being in the thick of having to manage my own change. It was 4 January 1994 and a snowy day, when we flew into Zagreb, in Croatia. This was going to be a completely new experience.

At this stage the British media had been covering the war in the former Yugoslavia for over two years and by their reckoning it was not a safe place to travel to. I arrived imagining the worst and looking over my shoulder fearful of gunmen on every street corner.

During the first few days, I just wanted to go home. I felt lonely, and missed the familiarity of my home, friends and family. Now it was replaced with a completely different life. We were initially staying in a hotel that also housed many refugees and their families from the conflict. There was an air of sadness and depression around the hotel and the bare white walls of my former Eastern bloc style of hotel bedroom became unbearable.

But after a few days I looked around at the others who had started working the same day, and I thought to myself, if they can stay then so can I. Why was I not handling this well?

It's so easy to get caught in a comfortable life that when you get jolted out of it the change can be difficult to manage. I had to remind myself why I was there. What was the vision? I wanted to be an adventurer, and this was about as adventurous as you could get.

Kickstart Tip

Maintain focus

You need to keep your own vision in mind when the going gets tough. Remind yourself of the reason that you are facing these challenges.

Being True to Your Values and Beliefs

After several weeks I had found a comfortable apartment. It was close to the river and an impressive sports facility that had been built for the World Student Games held in Zagreb several years earlier. Gradually life began to improve. The reality of living in Zagreb was just like most other large cities. There were no gunmen standing on each street corner, nor was there a real sense of threat that many people can feel in large cities like New York or London late at night.

Work, however, was a continual challenge. Having gone from an organization that was run pretty well to one where the word 'efficiency' did not seem to exist made life frustrating. Even though we were operating in a war zone, trying to improve the lives of the people who worked and lived there, bureaucracy reared its ugly head regularly. I began to realize just why so many people had introduced their own ways of working, because the UN system just did not seem effective even if it had been used. The flexibility that companies need to display if they want to survive that was described earlier did not seem to exist within this organization.

Ironically different nationalities seemed to migrate into different types of jobs. For example, the Engineering function was staffed mostly by Australians and Americans who operated with their own systems and procedures imported from those countries. Trying to encourage people to change to the 'UN way' was like trying to push water uphill.

So not only was life outside of work tough to get used to, but within work it was not easy either. I began to realize that the only way to make real progress that would make a positive difference was to work with the people that wanted to change and hope that it would create a snowball effect.

Many organizations experience this situation when they are trying to implement a culture change. If there is no commitment from the top of the organization, then any change initiative is likely to fail. How the senior people *behave* is noticed more than what they *say*, so if they espouse values about equality, for example, and then barge to the front of the queue in the canteen, the behaviour speaks volumes and the rest of the organization will not take their words seriously. Actions definitely speak louder than words.

That year in the former Yugoslavia was a constant learning experience. Not only did I learn about how organizations as large and as complicated as the United Nations work or don't work as efficiently as they could do, I learnt about how to be true to my own values and beliefs. Even though we had made progress in a small way with some departments, there was still a lack of commitment from those in the senior positions in terms of taking action. Therefore I felt it no longer tenable to be paid for trying to improve efficiency when there was no apparent real commitment to do so by the organization.

As described in Chapter 1, one of the components of Learned Powerfulness™ is Authenticity. If you truly want to remain motivated for a long period of time, and be prepared to face all types of challenges, you need to be true to your own values and beliefs. The first step is to work out for you what you truly believe in and are passionate about. That will help to guide you on your journey towards success.

When the one-year contract had been completed, I came back to the UK. This was the time I had feared the most because

I had no job. Strangely enough, rather than feeling scared, I now felt that the world was my oyster and there were a myriad of things I could do. I felt calm, yet excited. Eventually I decided to go back to university and complete my Masters Degree course in Quality Management on a full-time basis. I had already begun it on a part-time basis and had been studying for two years, and this seemed like an ideal time to complete it.

Studying was hard work, but as a mature student I revelled in it, because this time I was motivated to learn whereas at school I was there because I had to be. There seemed to be no time for thinking about the future, but my subconscious mind was still at work, and was not going to let any opportunities pass me by.

Summary

1. Consider how any major new learning experience will be integrated into 'normal life'.
2. A greater commitment to change will be likely if there is an element of choice.
3. We can help ourselves to grow and develop by helping others.
4. Measure the effectiveness of your decision making based on gut-feel.
5. When fear threatens to quash your motivation, maintain your vision to remind yourself of why you are changing.
6. You can only truly feel happy in an organization when their values and beliefs match your own.

Chapter 4

The Ultimate Challenge

In this chapter we examine:

- Comfort zones
- Commitment
- Physical and mental fitness
- Team development

Throughout this book I have talked about taking small steps to success, and building upon the success of one risk and then stretching your comfort zone further. This has two benefits in terms of your motivation:

(1) It keeps you continually focusing on another goal and can help to keep you motivated.
(2) Your level of confidence increases such that a challenge that appeared impossible earlier may now seem achievable.

This chapter addresses both of the points above in that it is the account of the 'Ultimate Challenge' expedition to the Magnetic North Pole which only appeared possible in 1995 taking into consideration the steps that had been taken as outlined in Chapters 2 and 3. Have you ever imagined what surviving in the Arctic is like? Imagine facing polar bears, temperatures cold enough to freeze your flesh in seconds, and trekking for up to eight hours a day while pulling a load heavier than the weight of an average man!

The following words featured in the newspaper that I was reading in my garden in the summer of 1995. Lounging on the chair, it was hard to imagine what that type of environment must be like, considering it was about 27°C at that time. But the feature went on to say . . .

'WANTED ten novice arctic explorers' – to take part in an expedition to walk 350 miles to the Magnetic North Pole.

There were two qualifications that the organizers required. The first was the ability to work in a team, and the second, the ability to raise £15 000. I knew that I could work in a team, having been on the Operation Raleigh expedition, but I had absolutely no idea how raising that amount of money would be possible. The only experience I had to go on was the £1500 raised for the Operation Raleigh expedition in 1988. But this was a whole different ballgame as there was another zero on the end of the sum required!

Kickstart Tip

Become aware of the messages you tell yourself

- What would you think if you had read the advertisement?
- Would it have seemed possible or unachievable or even unappealing?
- What would you be saying to yourself at this time? Notice what your reaction was when you read the previous paragraph.

I read the story with interest and then continued to browse through the newspaper. Later that evening, my subconscious must have been at work, and something drew me back to the newspaper and to that story. At the foot of the page was a telephone number to call for more details of the expedition.

When we are faced with potential opportunities like this, people tend to base their decisions on experience and what they feel is within their own limits of possibility. There is also that little voice inside all of us that speaks in your ear and whispers phrases like 'Don't be silly, you would never be able to do that', or 'What makes you think that you could ever raise £15 000? That's the deposit for buying a house, or it could be the cost of a flashy car.' How often do you listen to your inner voice and not accept a new challenge? Perhaps one of the reasons is that as we get older, our belief in our own potential seems to diminish, or maybe the voice inside us gets louder!

What happens to make us change? When we are children, we tend to think we are capable of anything, yet, as we get older and learn more about our capabilities, we put barriers in the way, and stop ourselves from really testing our abilities. These barriers, I believe, are the sum total of our life's experiences and the zone of relative comfort with which we surround ourselves.

This zone includes things that we are familiar with and feel comfortable with, such as our home, family, friends, tasks that we can accomplish easily etc. However, if we want to undertake a new challenge it means stepping outside this zone into a previously undiscovered area of learning.

Inhibiting Factors

What are the factors that encourage us to come out of our comfort zone and learn more about what we can be truly capable of? David Whitaker, the former coach to the Great Britain men's hockey team, in his book *The Spirit of Teams* suggests that there can be several reasons that inhibit individuals from expanding their comfort zone. These are issues such as fear of failure, low confidence, low self-worth and previous negative experiences. He calls these *internal blockages* because they are inner beliefs that are within our own control and are not easily managed by anyone else.

However, if we feel we can test ourselves, stretch our abilities and are encouraged perhaps by a coach or a friend, these internal blockages can be overcome. This is achieved by encouraging the spirit of 'I can' within the person. These blockages can also be overcome by also addressing what might motivate an individual to *want* to step outside their comfort zone. David Whitaker called these the *motivating factors*.

Motivating Factors

Motivating factors could be described as those elements that encourage us to want to try something new. These factors include:

- Because we want to improve our performance at something
- Because we enjoy taking part in a particular activity and we want to improve to the next level of competence
- Because as people we have an inherent drive to learn

Kickstart Tip

> ### Enjoyment and learning
>
> When we are *enjoying* a particular activity or environment, we can move outside our comfort zone. Back in the workplace, if we *enjoy* what we do, we are often willing to stretch ourselves or learn new skills or take on a more demanding role because we feel we are capable of doing so.
>
>   When we *learn*, we also have to move out of our comfort zone. When you learnt to drive imagine how difficult it felt the first time, but we persevere through the discomfort in order to learn.

So in the case of this opportunity to take part in an Arctic expedition, I wanted to *learn*. I wanted to know if it was an environment I could survive in, and what this polar region was like. There was no reason to delay. Next day I rang the number to get more information.

Negative Motivation Can Work Too

When the brochure arrived a few days later, it showed a picture of some adventurers skiing across the icecap, dragging sledges. But the most significant thing to hit me was the words on the front page. Are you *man* enough for the Ultimate Challenge?

Immediately my mind raced back to books I had read all those years ago as a child about Sir Edmund Hillary, Sir Chay Blyth or

Cook and Peary's race to the North Pole – all those *men* who had been successful adventurers. This statement shouted out to me that the organizers of this trip were under the same assumption as I had been as a youngster. Only men could be successful adventurers. I was incensed. Suddenly that became the motivation, albeit in a negative form, that I needed to follow this through. I'll show them I thought to myself. If they think only men can do this, I am going to prove them wrong.

The application form had no difficult questions, just the standard type asking why you should be the one to be selected and asking you to explain what qualities you had that were appropriate for this expedition. I had no trouble completing the form, knowing that my Operation Raleigh experience would be extremely valuable. However, I began to worry about what other types of people would apply, and whether they would be more experienced.

Making a Commitment

Another factor shrewdly included by the organizers was the small sum of £75 that had to be returned with your application. This would be taken from the overall sum if you were successful. At this time in 1995 this amount was a lot of money, because I was a lowly student. However, I decided that it was worth it, because I knew that this was not the type of chance that came up too often. So I typed the application and sent it off. I know that the organizers received over 800 enquiries and this was reduced to about 500 applications. Perhaps having to make a financial commitment really sorted out who was truly committed to getting on the team?

Selecting the Team

If you were responsible for selecting a team for an Arctic expedition, what qualities would you look for in your team members? You might think that the organizers would be looking for hardy types, with great map reading and first-aid skills, or people who had climbed mountains or successfully undertaken feats of derring-do.

In fact, the qualities that they were looking for were:

- Determination
- Enthusiasm
- A sense of humour
- A person who would look out for the other team members when the going got tough
- Someone who could communicate effectively with others.

In the business world employers are looking for similar qualities from the potential candidates they seek to recruit. No longer are qualifications the only important element but the ability to work with others, to communicate and to be a team player also top the list of attributes that employers are looking for. It underlines how the challenges of the business world can often be equated with those of an extreme environment like the Arctic!

Five hundred people applied for the places, and the organizers narrowed it down initially to 40 people. We were all invited for a day of interviews and tests at a location in the south of England.

While driving there, I felt reasonably confident and once I had met the others, it seemed to me that they were just as experienced or inexperienced as I was, and so there was as much chance to be selected as the next person. Ironically at that stage, there were only around five women and some of them looked like they were more at home on the cover of a magazine rather than on an expedition – but you know what they say about not judging a book by its cover . . .

During the day, we also discovered that the BBC were going to be filming us and it would form part of a long-term relationship that they were to have with the expedition from selection to completion of the journey. This had not been mentioned in the information pack, and would make a significant difference for those who were selected in their quest for sponsorship. The idea of the company logo being seen on TV is a little more attractive to sponsors than just appearing in an outdoors magazine!

Kickstart Tip

Risk taking

It is not until you have taken a risk and opened the first door that you are able to see the opportunities beyond which may help you on the journey towards your goal.

During this initial session, we learnt more about the plans for the expedition, and were shown some slides from previous journeys in the Arctic in which the organizers David Hempleman-Adams and Jock Wishart had taken part.

David Hempleman-Adams is a well-known polar adventurer who along with Jock Wishart and three others, Neill Williams,

Richard Mitchell, and Hugh Ward, had skied to the Geomagnetic North Pole in 1992. This current expedition was the brainchild of Jock and David, and they were keen to discover if it was possible to undertake such a feat with a group of novices.

Selection was one of the most significant elements to ensure a successful expedition and great care had been taken to devise a method that would try to address any potential weaknesses within the final team.

We had to undertake a series of physical and mental tests including the notorious assault course at Sandhurst, the military college in the UK. Having a fear of heights, I was sure that this test, which has several high obstacles, would single me out as a failure. However, after the first race around it, I realized that again the organizers were not looking for our skills as individuals, but how well we worked together as a team. This was lucky because when we reached the 10-metre high cargo net and had to climb over the top of it, I just froze and was petrified to lift my feet from one side of the net and put them on the other.

The others in our group came to my rescue and with lots of encouragement I gingerly lifted my legs over the top and onto the other side. After that encounter the next obstacle was just as challenging. It was a narrow brick wall to walk along that just happened to be 5 metres from the ground with a gap in the middle! In a strange sort of way I really enjoyed the event, and at the end felt even more confident knowing that I had a realistic chance of making the final ten.

A month later, our next test was planned. This time it was a 28-mile walk along part of the Ridgeway, which is Britain's oldest road that stretches across the south-west of England from near the River Thames to the Chiltern Hills. Jock told us that the walking pace would be 4 miles an hour, and as we were walking in December with limited daylight we would aim to begin at 8.30 am and it should take us 7 hours. This was a tough target to set, and although I had packed my day rucksack as if on a picnic, with sandwiches and coffee, I soon realized that there was going to be no time for breaks, let alone trying to scoff a sandwich!

By this stage in the selection process, the organizers had narrowed the numbers down to fourteen of us, and there were now twelve men and two women. Susanna Wikman, who was the other female, was Swedish, but lived and worked in London as an office manager. Susanna and I had hit it off from the first time we had met, and I felt pleased that she was still in the selection process for the team. As we walked together, we talked about our fears and hopes for the expedition. Both Susanna and I had discussed any potential problems that we felt we might encounter from being female and we both agreed there were not really any major challenges that we had not already faced in our personal or working lives.

We all appeared fit and healthy for the first few miles and the fast pace was maintained easily. Then by mid-afternoon, around the 15-mile stage, the wear and tear began to show on some of the team. Simon Marshall and Mike Piercy dropped back because both of them were suffering from some type of injury. This immediately became obvious and was noted by Jock who was eagerly watching how we all performed. We took it in turns to navigate as well, although as we were walking along a well-worn Roman road, it was none too challenging.

As the afternoon wore on, and the light began to fade, so did our energy levels. There was a quieter, more sombre mood among the group, as people focused their energies on just putting one foot in front of the other. It was interesting to watch people struggle mentally and when they were asked how they were doing, they would immediately answer 'fine!' without question, as if that was the only answer allowed.

The BBC film crew had also been following us, mostly in a vehicle and would speed ahead to film us coming over the next rise, or down the next lane. As we neared the end of our trek, it was now completely dark, and we had to walk a mile or so, down a tarmac lane back to the pub that was our start and finish point. This was hell on the legs, as the pain from this arduous day seemed even greater when our legs hit the hard, concrete surface. Jock then finally shouted to us, as we neared the end, to break into a jog, so that we could film it for TV. Our legs screamed even more, and we all must have looked as if we had jelly legs as we wobbled our way to the end. We were all so glad to see the end, the warmth of the pub and a decent meal. Now another stage in the selection process was over.

It was now only four months to the start of the expedition, and we were all furiously trying to fund-raise on the assumption that we were all going to be selected. After all, if we left it until we knew that we had been definitely chosen, and then we could face the prospect of being in the team, but not being able to participate through lack of funds.

Raising the Bar

Have you ever had to fund-raise for a worthy cause? As mentioned in Chapter 2, it can really help to have some passion for what you are doing. When you truly believe in what you are fund-raising for, it comes through in the conversations that you have with people, and they are more likely to be sympathetic to your cause. Without the passion that comes from belief and a determination to achieve whatever it is you are fund-raising for it is much more difficult to be successful.

I had no previous experience of raising this amount of money but I knew that in order to get sponsorship it was going to require media involvement. Now that the BBC was committed to covering our expedition, this was a big bonus, and enabled all of us to attract more interest, especially when companies knew that their brand name or logo might be seen on our clothing on the news. It seemed is if this was stepping into the premier league in terms of raising sponsorship and therefore I had to seek help from friends that I thought knew more about this than I did.

Together we brainstormed all the names of organizations or companies who had some link to the cold environment or people that I knew who could perhaps help. We then created a letter to send to them stating what benefits they could expect to receive if they became a sponsor of the expedition.

This was a massive gamble, as I had to state that I was confident of being selected even though the final decision had not been taken. The week before Christmas, my fears were laid to rest. Jock rang me to say that I had been selected as one of the ten in the team. Although I was delighted, the selection process had been so prolonged that we had all almost begun to imagine that we were in the team anyway. It was obviously much more distressing for those who were not chosen to take part, having put so much time and effort into the process.

Kickstart Tip

> ## Togetherness
>
> Consideration must always be given to the 'goodbye' process in teams. It is important to ensure that those who are not continuing in the team feel good about leaving and are treated fairly and with empathy. That way they are more likely to retain their self-esteem and dignity.

Susanna had also been chosen, and I was extremely pleased to have another female on the team, as I felt sure that there would be some situations we could encounter where it would be beneficial to have another female.

This now meant that I could go full steam ahead on fundraising. I had already received several negative responses to my letters for sponsorship. However, with the holiday season about to start, I decided that this was not really the time that companies were going to be interested in sponsorship deals, more like Christmas parties!

Targeting Companies for Funding

I headed off to Slovenia for Christmas and enjoyed a relaxing few days skiing and hiking in the snow-covered mountains. On my return to the hotel one afternoon, I called home to discover that there was a letter from Bird's Eye stating that they were interested in the expedition and were potentially sponsoring a place. My heart leapt, as this was the first real positive news I had received from a company. Immediately I rang them and arranged a meeting with them on my return to the UK.

It just seemed too good to be true that not more than one week after confirmation of my place on the team, there was a possibility of getting started on the road to success.

That was the break I needed, and following the meeting with Bird's Eye, they agreed to sponsor the entire amount of £15 000. In return, I agreed to carry out several presentations to schools on my return from the Arctic to promote their Bird's Eye Schools Education Pack. I also agreed to wear their logo on my clothing, which would have a good chance of appearing on BBC TV as the likelihood of the reporters wanting to interview the females on the team was fairly high!

If you are going to approach companies for sponsorship, they will always want to know how they will benefit immediately. Most companies receive thousands of enquiries each year and almost all end up in the bin, particularly if the letter is not addressed to anyone in particular or the name has been spelled incorrectly.

Kickstart Tip

Tips on getting sponsorship

My experience has been that companies will rarely read more than one page of text, and it should include:

- Why they should read the letter (what is different about your project)
- The goal of the project
- What you actually want (specific help to fund a particular item)
- What's in it for them (features and benefits)?
- How much will it cost?
- How you will contact them to follow up?

Good preparation before you even send out a letter is required. It is worth researching who in the company should receive such a request, which can be done by an initial phone call. It also pays to keep up-to-date with current news so that you are not approaching a company that has just announced redundancies or are relocating their headquarters to the USA!

Effective Preparation and Planning

Regardless of whether you are planning an expedition to the Arctic or planning to achieve a sales target in business, effective preparation and planning are two of the factors that are critical to success.

It is key that you clearly understand what your vision is (i.e. a picture of what you want to achieve) and truly understand what success means for you. If you do not know what you are really trying to achieve, then you will never be sure if you have achieved it. Simple really, but so often people think they know what they are doing, but they have not thought about what it actually means in great detail. Understanding the vision is a key element in creating your own success.

Our vision was to get to the Magnetic North Pole in one piece, with no injuries and as a team. The biggest factor that was out of our control was the weather and it would be the most likely thing to stop us. However, there were many other things that were within our control that could impact on our success. These were:

- how well we worked as a team
- our physical fitness
- our mental ability to withstand the tough environment
- how we would overcome our fears and worries

Team Development

There are several different stages of development that teams experience as they move towards achieving their goal. Dr Alan Beggs in *The Human Dimension* has developed a five-stage model for team development called Team Powerfulness, which corresponds with the levels within Maslow's hierarchy of needs model (Figure 4.1). The difference between the two is that the latter describes the needs of an individual and the Team

Powerfulness model translates these needs into the emotional needs for a team. This model correlates with Daniel Goleman's work on Emotional Intelligence where he also indicates that successful teams and individuals are able to manage their emotions effectively as well as using their cognitive intelligence. A team that does not address emotional issues is unlikely to be able to perform at a high level.

The stages of the Team Powerfulness model move from *Embryonic* to *Dynamic*. Each level requires the team to meet the differing emotional needs of each individual within it, e.g. *Embryonic* is when a team are attempting to establish their social needs (the first level of Maslow's model). Once they are met they move onto satisfying their status needs, then self-esteem needs, then self-actualization for each team member and finally when they are no longer focused on emotional needs within the team, they are able to operate at a level of peak performance. This state of being a *dynamic* team is not sustainable continuously and most teams never reach it. However, I am sure that every person has experienced that feeling of effortlessness, feeling powerful, invincible and having a sense of meaning and purpose within what they do at some time in their lives.

The Team Powerfulness model identifies the emotions that need to be addressed at each stage of team development before the team can move forward together to the next level. If one person in the team fails to have their needs met at that particular level, then the team itself will not develop to the next level. This model moves forward from the descriptive model of Forming, Storming, Norming and Performing that Tuckman developed in the 1960s. Tuckman's model did not explain how

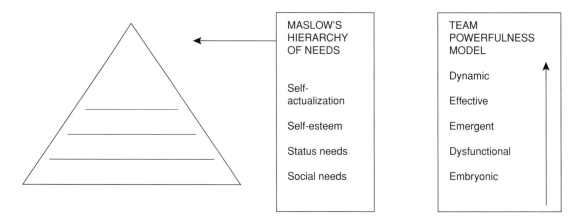

Figure 4.1   The Team Powerfulness model compared with Maslow's hierarchy of needs

the teams were able to move from one level to the next whereas the Team Powerfulness model clearly shows how this this development can be achieved.

Embryonic Teams

The first stage of development is an *embryonic* team and this was happening during the months prior to the expedition, when the selection phase was taking place. It is during this phase in a team that the individual energy within the team is focused inwardly, and each person wants to feel included and part of the team as a whole (social needs). Conflict on the whole does not arise as individuals are trying to be nice to one another.

Dysfunctional Teams

After the team was narrowed down, we slowly began to learn more about one another, and understand what each individual's strengths and weaknesses were. This moved us into the *dysfunctional* stage. Conflict situations can arise, several times and this can indicate in a team that people are trying to meet their own status needs, i.e. people are feeling they need to be valued and recognized for their contribution to the team.

We had all completed a questionnaire that looked at our own personality styles and analysed how we would operate in stressful situations. We discussed the results in small groups with the help of a facilitator. That way we were able to look at the results objectively and understand more about one another.

A group of people cannot be transformed into an effective team unless they are committed to going through these various stages of development. Sometimes tough talking is needed, and at other times empathy and support, but most of all a common goal must be established, so at least everyone understands what they are working together to achieve.

As such, there is no way that as a group of ten novices we would have been able to reach the Pole without any leadership or supervision. There was a lot we had to learn about surviving in the Arctic and one factor that would help us more than anything else was our willingness to work together to achieve our aim. That way if the going got tough, we would feel safe and secure within the group and not worry that everyone was out for themselves only and not concerned about the needs of the others.

We decided to meet regularly prior to the expedition not only to discuss the individual tasks that we were allocated to arrange but also to give ourselves a chance to get to know one another. On one occasion, we went walking in a forest, on another we met in a pub in the evening. All these activities were useful in developing shared understanding and trust and moving us to the next level on the Beggs' team model.

Emergent Teams

Each person was allocated a responsibility within the overall expedition. My role was to co-ordinate the media coverage that we obtained to ensure that we had copies of all newspaper or magazine articles that featured expedition members. That way we could assess the benefits that sponsors accrued from their contributions. Other roles that people had were navigation, food and first aid. Our regular fortnightly meetings were designed to ensure we were all confident that the others were progressing their particular areas of responsibility. During these meetings, we began to move into the next phase of the team development model known as *emergent*. Individuals began to feel valued, they understood the responsibilities they had, and also how they fitted into the team as a whole.

Effective Teams

We also all knew that once we were out in the Arctic, we would all have to work together as a highly *effective* team. By working to understand what would motivate each person to realize their own objectives from the expedition in addition to our team goals, we felt that this would enable us to truly be effective together. Some people wanted to appreciate the environment whereas others wanted a tough physical challenge. Teams who attain peak performance have to work at it, and that is not always easy particularly in stressful environments.

Dynamic Teams

Our expedition team was rarely able to perform at the level where everything felt effortless and each individual felt personally powerful and invincible. This was not because we were ineffective, but rather that this state is difficult to attain simultaneously within each team member. The process known as *Learned Powerfulness*™ ultimately produces the level of performance that was described in Chapter 1. It is realistic to develop the capability to be full of power and energy, yet it will only be experienced sporadically, and most teams are unaware of how to achieve this state in a more sustained manner.

Kickstart Tip

Developing teams

Addressing the emotional needs within a team will enable it to develop much more quickly than just working on the task issues.

Physical Fitness

An expedition that involves skiing for up to 10 hours a day is fairly physical! Therefore it is vital that those participating are physically able to endure that level of exercise day after day. The organizers had already used physical tests as part of the selection process, and had ensured that we all had a basic level of fitness. Now it was down to each individual to prepare in the most appropriate manner.

Being a reasonably fit person anyway, and having trained for years in athletics, I was used to doing some form of physical exercise every day. However, this training was going to have to be more focused and specifically designed to develop stamina and endurance – the two qualities needed to be able to ski vast distances every day. An all-round level of fitness would be more beneficial than having bulging arm or leg muscles.

My fitness plan involved a variety of different activities. Every week there would be at least two gym sessions, which would be designed to develop endurance and stamina. Activities such as repeatedly lifting easy weights are better than short heavy jerks to develop muscles like a weightlifter.

I also did several long runs at a fairly easy pace, plus swimming to continue developing the stamina. David Hempleman-Adams had told us that we all needed to know how to ski, and although I had never cross-country skied prior to this expedition, I was a reasonable downhill skier.

As you will begin to understand, to have the best chance of success we had to be well prepared for everything, but not necessarily an expert in any one area. Being a highly tuned athlete might have actually been a hindrance. If you had tuned up specific muscles in the gym, and then used them continuously in a different movement like skiing, then there could be an increased danger of pulling a muscle.

Some of the other team members were not able to undertake a rigorous fitness regime and felt at a disadvantage prior to the start of the journey. If our expedition was going to suffer because of this lack of preparation, this problem would only show itself once we got out there and began to get physically exhausted.

Kickstart Tip

Benefits of exercise

Even in business these days the philosophy of 'healthy body, healthy mind' is taken seriously. Large corporations are encouraging their staff to visit the gym or undertake some form of exercise. It is ironic that even though we imagine exercise will tire us, it can invigorate and can help staff to refocus after a lunchtime swim or workout.

For our team, it was going to become what we did all day, every day, and we had to be able to cope with that prospect.

As well as being physically fit, we also had to ensure we would have enough body fat to cope with the cold. Our diet would be at least 5000 calories per day because we would be pulling heavy sleds and facing temperatures of –40°C and we would also need to have enough body fat to maintain warmth. David

Hempleman-Adams had put on nearly 14 lbs before his 600-mile South Pole expedition in 1995 and although our journey was not going to be as tough as that, it did mean eating all the things that normally we are told are not healthy. We could eat cookies, chips, and chocolate and all in large portions. It was the best Christmas I ever had, knowing it was acceptable to over-indulge.

There was, however, a corollary to this. If you are trying to do more physical exercise and increase your food intake at the same time, it becomes tough. All the extra exercise means that you are hungry, and all the extra food is used to replace the burnt-up calories, so you then need to eat even more food. Sometimes we would resort to ridiculous situations in order to get extra calories like eating chocolate sponge pudding with custard made from Jersey cream milk that contained extra fat. It was a hard life!

Mental Strength

Building up mental strength is something that most sane people would probably never dream of doing. For our impending adventure it was a quality that would be critical to our success. Perhaps it's something that you either have or you don't and I did not really think too seriously at this stage about how to develop it.

What I did think about was how I had survived on previous occasions in challenging environments, and by knowing that, I was able to convince myself that I could survive in the Arctic. The most critical factor on this expedition was going to be having the passion and determination to achieve our vision. I believed that if I was sufficiently prepared physically, then it would help to develop my mental strength and belief in what I was planning to do. It's very hard to imagine skiing for 10 hours a day, for a month, when you have never cross-country skied before and never dragged a sledge either. However, overcoming that little voice in your head that introduces negative thoughts is the first step.

Another way to develop mental strength is to think about any challenging situation you have been in or seen others in. Maybe it was an emergency situation, where people carried out feats that they never dreamed of. A TV documentary by survival expert Ray Mears told the story of a young couple who survived for a month in the Arctic when experts believed they were only capable of surviving for the maximum of a week. The single most important quality that helped them was belief. They always believed that they would be rescued and they never let any negative thoughts enter their heads. This must have been the same for Ernest Shackleton's crew who were stranded on Elephant Island in the Antarctic while they waited for him to come back and rescue them after their ill-fated polar expedition in 1914.

When we are in any challenging situation or new environment we can feel fear. It can be fear of the unknown, or fear that we do not have the ability. Think of an athlete lining up to race against people who are normally faster than him or her. If they focus on past performance or on the other athletes, the mental game is lost as the mind set is possibly that the others are better or faster. However, if they focus on thinking positively and on the thoughts that help them as opposed to hindering them, then the mental battle can be won. It is extremely difficult at times. The little negative voice inside our heads can often have a louder volume than the positive one!

Kickstart Tip

Mind games

In a race against others, focus your mind on your own performance and what you can do to improve it. *You* control your thoughts and actions and if you are worrying about the competition, then you are not able to focus on your own plan of action. The competitors may affect your plan, but you cannot control their actions so focus on what you can control.

This was my approach to our Arctic expedition. I thought about what the worst things might be – falling through the ice, being eaten by a bear, being stuck in the same tent with people you don't get on with for the whole time, or not washing for a month? Then I thought about what I could do to address these situations and if they were not within my control then there was no point in worrying about them. Just being mentally prepared to know what to do if these situations arose was most important. That's where having others in our team really helped. I was able to trust that the others would also be able to help in the event of falling in the ice or getting frostbite.

Addressing the 'What if' Scenarios

Many of the fears I had were also shared by others in the team. We decided that it was most appropriate to address these fears before we even reached the ice and to do that we should talk about them together.

That takes courage and an environment of trust. By the time we had all been through selection together and worked on our individual roles and met regularly we had a pretty good trusting environment. We then met together to address some of our fears. Everyone asked questions like 'What if someone gets injured, will we all have to give up?' and 'What if we can't walk at the pace required?' or 'What if our equipment fails?' or 'How will we communicate with the outside world?' For those in the team with spouses or partners, there were also the fears that the other partner needed to have addressed to ensure that the one actually going felt more confident in the knowledge that their partner's fears were allayed.

To achieve this, we also held a couple of events where partners attended too, and they were able to meet the other team members and ask questions. During that occasion, I did feel that some of the other team member's partners were eyeing Susanna and I jealously and wondering if their husbands would be safe in this female company. Never mind the men, I felt that at least with two of us, we had some safety in numbers! Although relationships have been known to strike up when people work closely together I could not imagine anything like that happening in a freezing tent in the High Arctic! I believed that all of us, no matter what gender we were, had the determination and commitment to get there, to be successful and not to allow any factor to get in the way of our vision.

All these methods of preparation are just as valuable in the business world. The staff need to know what is expected of them, what they are committing to, and what might be the drawbacks or problems. Employers need to find a way of addressing the fears and concerns of staff, while helping to encourage them to become responsible for their own physical and mental state within the workplace. If a person is not focused on what they are working at, they are less likely to be performing to the best of their abilities. Again these emotional issues that were described earlier by Daniel Goleman as being key to peak performance play a part in how staff perform effectively.

After four months of preparation our expedition team felt physically and mentally ready to face our Ultimate Challenge. And by now if you have been developing your own capabilities too, it will only be a matter of time to see if all these preparations are going to be beneficial . . .

Summary

1. Fear, a lack of confidence, and lack of self-belief are some of the factors that may inhibit people from expanding their comfort zone.
2. Our desire to improve performance and the pleasure of learning a new skill can be factors that motivate us to expand our comfort zone.
3. Be aware of what motivates you. Is it positive encouragement (you can do it) or negative criticism (you'll never be able to do that)?

4. Will you put 'your money where your mouth is' when tested on your level of commitment to your goal? If not, ask yourself, what is stopping me from doing this?

5. The qualities needed to be successful in the Arctic or any other physically or mentally challenging environment are similar to those required to survive in today's business world.

6. When stretching your capabilities, think creatively for solutions. They can appear in mysterious ways if you are open to new ideas.

7. Time spent on preparation when fund-raising, will reap rewards in the long run. You need to address the sponsors' question 'What's in it for me?'

8. Focus on what you *do* have control over rather than what you do not.

9. A team is only as effective as the people within it. Individuals must have their own emotional needs met at each stage of the process if the team is to grow and develop. Managing your emotions effectively is key to peak performance.

10. Appropriate physical *and* mental preparations are critical for success in both adventure and business.

11. Nobody likes surprises and if you have thought about the 'what if?' options before the situation arises, then it can be less stressful.

Chapter 5

Stepping into the Unknown

In this chapter we examine:

- Goal setting
- Communication
- Diversity
- Leadership styles

The process of challenging yourself to find out what you are capable of can be never-ending. Certainly that's how I felt when we began the main part of our journey to the Magnetic North Pole in 1996. This chapter describes that expedition and how our team was able to challenge and overcome our own self-limiting beliefs to achieve our goal. It also enables the reader to draw analogies between our experiences and those that business people encounter frequently in the workplace.

8 April 1996 – The fateful day dawned bright and early when it was time to leave on the Ultimate Challenge expedition. Three of us were travelling together five days earlier than the main party. That way we could prepare some of the equipment in advance and ensure that the few days the entire team had together at our base camp were used most effectively.

It was a long flight from London via Edmonton and Calgary in Canada to Resolute Bay in Canada's Nunavut Territory. Resolute is Canada's second most northerly community and the start-point for most Arctic expeditions. Only around 400 people live here with the main Inuit community situated 4 miles from the airport. When we arrived the pilot announced that it was –20°C and as we looked out of the windows we could see a desolate landscape devoid of life and trees below us. I still could not really believe that we were going to be trying to survive in this wilderness for almost a month!

We received a warm welcome from the woman who ran the High Arctic boarding house – a glorified bed and breakfast which is homely and comfortable and provides plenty of wholesome food that would-be explorers thrive on in these cold conditions. She took us back to the house, which is in the town, and gave us tea and cakes, which were just perfect.

Already at the camp were several other expedition parties, either returning from hunting trips or preparing for their own expeditions. The atmosphere around the dinner table was lively with conversation mainly focusing on what each team was planning to do. Although there was not really any competition between each group, there was also an air of uncertainty, with the others not giving too much away.

The following days were spent organizing some of the equipment that had already arrived and building an insulated sled that would contain the entire camera and satellite equipment that would be carried with us by the BBC engineer.

By the time the others arrived five days later, we had already begun to get used to the way of life at the bed and breakfast place and were able to help the others to settle in much more quickly. Even if you were going outside for only a few minutes, care had to be taken to wear the appropriate amount of clothing and always gloves and a hat. It's amazing just how quickly you can get cold and that's how frostbite can take hold of people.

The livelihood of the inhabitants of Resolute is hunting and providing outfitter services to the hunters and adventurers that come to the High Arctic in search of caribou, polar bears and adventure.

We began to try using our sledges and our cross-country skis. It was a strange sensation to try moving on skis while dragging a weight behind you. I was a little worried that this was what we were going to have to get used to for our expedition, especially having had no experience of this to date.

Our leader then announced to us all that we were going to take out all our equipment and tents that afternoon to just a few metres out of town and then set up camp and sleep for a night on the ice. That way the following day we could ski back to the hotel and make any adjustments to our equipment that were needed.

Kickstart Tip

Benefits of testing

- Pilot exercises can provide valuable learning and reduce rework time.
- People are more likely to be supportive if you are honest with them about the fact it's a test situation.
- Ask for their feedback so you can learn and improve and they will feel involved.

By now there were sixteen of us at the camp – ten novices, four leaders, and a BBC engineer. Our sleeping arrangements were four people to a tent, which included one leader and three novices. The tenth novice would sleep in a tent with the two people who were responsible for media. They were going to be sending regular reports back to the media and the cameraman's job was to take plenty of interesting footage to be able to send back via satellite for the weekly update on the BBC breakfast news programmes. Therefore the person sharing this tent was going to be at a slight disadvantage because there would be a lot more equipment in the tent, and obviously a lot more activity with the two of them working on their handheld computers all evening.

The plan was for each person to share another tent with a different tent leader after a week on the ice, and that way we hoped to avoid cliques developing within the group.

I felt excited that first evening as we all walked slowly out across the ice to an area just a few yards from the last houses in town. Dragging our sledges with all the equipment in made it extremely heavy going, and I began to worry that it would prove impossible to carry all this weight on the actual journey. At least we would have a chance to ditch unwanted items before we left properly.

We took at least twenty minutes to erect the tents and it was lucky that it was calm, as otherwise we would all have got rather cold. There is a set routine that is required to set up the tent, and once you have established what each individual's role is in this routine, it makes the whole operation that much quicker.

One person takes responsibility for each side of the tent and puts in the poles at the same time as the person on the opposite end. Once all the poles are in place, the skis are used like pegs to keep the tent in place, and then snow is shovelled on the valance that surrounds the tent rather like a skirt. This stops any wind getting under the tent and uprooting it.

Once the tent has been secured with the skis, the other team members have other jobs to do. One person gets inside the tent and lays out the camping mats in a line together while another is outside putting more snow on the valance of the tent. Once the tent is laid out properly inside, then one person outside passes all the items required for the evening to the person inside such as a sleeping bag, spare clothing, personal items, food, the stove and fuel etc. Once you have been sharing a tent with the same people for a few days, you get to know what equipment needs to come inside, and the whole operation can be done that much quicker. This may seem like a mundane activity but when the wind is blowing and the temperature is about –40°C then any action must be carried out quickly to avoid getting cold.

Kickstart Tip

Advance planning

- Thinking ahead is critical to make sure that you have the key items required to achieve your goals ready ahead of time.
- This is critical in the business environment, particularly in high-risk ventures such as air traffic control, utilities such as gas or water and banking, where failure to get it right first time might be catastrophic.
- 'What if' scenarios are useful to help focus thoughts on what might be the outcome of a particular situation. This enables more effective preparation for all possible situations that may impact your project.

Imagine that you are skiing along one day and you start to get really cold, and would like to put on another pair of gloves, or an extra hat. In a situation like that, you need to be able to locate these items quickly, and not take out all your equipment from your sledge and leave it strewn across the ice while you look for them. The danger is that your equipment could blow away, and that your fellow team members become cold and frustrated while they are waiting.

This attention to detail is also critical once you are out trekking each day. The part of your body most likely to get frostnip is your face, and it's the one part that you cannot see if it has lost circulation. Therefore, we all teamed up with another, and at each break in the day, we checked the face of our buddies to ensure that there were no small white patches appearing. These patches are the first sign of frostnip and attention must be paid to them immediately. By putting a warm hand straight onto the white area, heat can solve this problem. However, that particular area will then be more susceptible to frostnip in the future and it is important to cover it up if possible.

In business if small problems are left unattended, then a similar outcome can occur. Think of an office environment. John goes to use the photocopier, and the toner light is on, indicating that it is low. As John only has a few copies to make, he ignores this indicator, makes his copies and goes back to his desk. In the next office, Mary is finishing working on a large tender document and has 20 minutes to copy it and then send it out by the courier. She assumes that the photocopier will be working as usual, and is not feeling harassed at this stage. Once she prints the 10-page document, she heads off to the photocopier to make several copies. Half-way through the second run, the machine stops and the indicator light flashes, showing the toner-out sign. Of course, no one knows where the toner is stored and Mary is now panicking because time is running out and the courier will be arriving in a moment to collect this document.

Kickstart Tip

Attention to detail

- Lack of attention to detail could hinder the success of an entire business.
- Teamwork is critical even in an office environment with seemingly innocuous tasks. If these tasks are left undone, then the results can be devastating for everyone in terms of the team's ability to achieve their goals.
- Attention to detail as well as anticipating potential problems is therefore vital, and this quality can be invaluable in a team.

Using Expert Knowledge to Anticipate Potential Problems

Back in the UK, we all had our particular tasks to undertake to organize some of the equipment for this expedition. With no prior knowledge of how to survive in the Polar Regions, we relied on the expert leaders to tell us particular requirements for items of equipment. But with the best will in the world, team members had to be left to use their own best judgement too. It is very difficult to imagine how items of equipment might not work as you think they should, particularly in the cold or when you are wearing giant gloves that make your hands look like flippers.

Take, for example, the elastic cord that is normally found on the inner side of a tent pole that helps to join the separate pieces easily. It is the last thing that you would imagine could cause a problem out on the ice. However, in extreme temperatures the elastic loses its elasticity, and does not shrink, as you would expect. This means that it is extremely difficult to put the tent poles together as you are trying to stuff this cord into the pole. What makes it even more challenging is the fact that you have to be wearing gloves, as your hands must not touch the metal either!

In the warmth of a shop or your house, this small problem does not come to mind. Many other situations arise like this, when materials do not operate as you might expect them to in the cold.

The expertise and knowledge of someone who has been in that environment before is therefore critical. Too often, in the business world, we ignore similar experiences and get a person who has no idea of how an item will be used to purchase it. Agreeing the requirements becomes the most important element of this situation and the person making the purchase needs either to have a good understanding of what it will be used for or to be able to ask the appropriate type of questions, to get as much relevant information as possible. In the Arctic, the consequences are even more drastic and can be life-threatening.

We had to be on a steep learning curve during the first few days of being out on the ice. It was lucky that our leader, the experienced polar adventurer David Hempleman-Adams, had given us the opportunity to camp out close to Resolute. This meant that the following day we could head back to our base camp and make any changes to our equipment that we felt were appropriate.

I decided immediately that I would leave half of my gear at the base camp, because after the first night, all the items I thought would be essential suddenly did not now seem so, especially if they were going to have to be dragged over 350 miles!

So out went the spare pairs of socks, gloves, thermals, etc., and I was down to the bare minimum. I *did* choose to leave my book in as I felt it would be good to have something to read as an escape out on the ice. I had chosen the biography of 400-metre UK Olympic medallist Sally Gunnell, as I felt that when she was feeling that she was not able to achieve her goals in athletics, she must have found a way to overcome that mental obstacle. In reality I did find the book truly inspirational, giving me encouragement and determination to keep going, when I felt at my lowest.

It was a strange feeling, when we left to start on our journey to the Pole. We drove with all our sleds towards the airport to the nearest point that was flat and in the direction that we were headed and unloaded all the gear. Once we were clipped to the sledges, with skis on our feet, we left those who had come to wave us off behind. In a line, we snaked across the ice, one behind another, and it was scary to imagine that all that was now in front of us was ice. No people, no houses, just a bleak lifeless, cold environment where nature is in control in a place that wants you dead.

Goal Setting

We were all clear about what our goal was – to reach the Magnetic North Pole as a team. But to imagine that the final goal is 350 miles away is almost unbelievable, and is actually demotivating when all you think of is 349 miles to go, 348 miles to go . . .

We needed to have milestones in place as targets to aim for, and to help motivate us to think of the trip in smaller chunks that we could relate to more easily. That would help to give a day-to-day focus to the journey and maintain our levels of motivation.

So our first goal was the Polaris Mine, 65 miles away, or in our language, about 7 days' walking. This is the world's most northerly mine and around 100 workers spend a month at a time on shifts in this bleak part of the world. After that point, the next goal would be the top of Cornwallis Island, from where we would begin a trek across the MacLean Strait to the Noice Peninsula on Ellef Ringnes Island where the Magnetic Pole was located.

Kickstart Tip

Setting milestones

Break down your goals into smaller targets or milestones. That way it is more manageable to think about and easier to achieve and measure progress at each stage.

Even a target 7 days away was difficult to focus on so David our leader decided to give the task of managing each day to a different team. We were split into four teams of four people, our tent groups really, and each day a different group was given the responsibility for the route and the speed that we travelled.

This was extremely astute because it introduced an element of competition between each group. Team A would come up with their route and strategy for the day they managed. Our leader suggested that for the first few days we would gradually increase the number of sessions we walked from around five to eight. A session would last for an hour after which there would be a 5-minute break giving time for each person to pee, and get a hot drink and snack from their own bag of rations which were a mixture of high-energy snacks and chocolate.

This system meant that each day we were not really concerned with distances but with time. Although we were all eager to walk for more than five sessions on the first day, David sensibly stopped us to ensure that we did not use up all our energy or enthusiasm in the early part of the journey. The pace is often called the polar plod, as we did not move very quickly at all, around 3 or 4-kilometres per hour, but this is enough to conserve energy to ensure you make it through the day.

By day 5 or 6, the level of competition was increasing between the teams. The goal was to find the best pace to walk which would enable the entire group to cover the maximum distance per day. Team A would start off on their day in the lead, at an extremely fast pace. By sessions five or six, people would begin to be strung out across the ice, as their legs began to pay the price of the early fast pace. By the end of the day, the overall pace had dramatically slowed, and when our position was checked in the evening, by using a Global Positioning System (GPS) to locate our current position, the team would be able to calculate how far we had come. It would be around 13 miles.

Next day it was Team B's turn. This team decided to approach the day in a different way. They started off slowly with some of the others complaining because they were cold and it took them a long time to heat up. However, this tactic paid off because every-one was able to keep up this pace for longer. By the end of the day, fewer people were flagging and when the distance was measured on the GPS it was 14 miles. The team was jubilant.

This gave Team C more motivation for the following day, and so it went on. It was not always possible for each team to cover more mileage than the previous team's best because of conditions underfoot or the weather. However, it did serve as an excellent way to motivate the entire group. In a business environment the same can happen and the impact of this can be either beneficial or detrimental to the overall business, depending on how it is managed.

Kickstart Tip

Impact of competition between teams

- A friendly rivalry can motivate all teams to improve performance.
- It is important to establish overall goals that encourage teams to work together, e.g. a bonus being awarded for overall company performance, not departmental performance.
- Rewards that are focused only on individuals can lead to divisiveness rather than collaboration, because individuals can be unwilling to share learning or knowledge if they think that others will gain from it.

I have seen the downside of this competition happen within British Gas where the competition itself became more important than the goals of the business. They had a regional competition to measure levels of service. Competition was so fierce that employees were encouraged to ensure that all customers completed their customer-satisfaction forms, and even sometimes the employees would help them! Of course, several inventive methods were used to ensure that the results were as positive as possible. It would have been more helpful either to reward the most improving region or to ensure that it was the actual level of service that improved as opposed to the competition results!

One thing to encourage positive competition is to ensure that all the employees are aware of and truly understand the vision for an organization. If they understand it, and how what they do contributes to the overall success of the organization, then competition can help to motivate the employees as long as it is all aimed at moving towards the overall vision.

Routine Can Help People to Feel Comfortable and Safe

In business, regardless of how unique your job is, there are always some routines that people create because they provide a certain level of security and comfort in an ever-changing world. These routines can be as simple as always having coffee with your colleagues at a certain time, or having a framework for your day, for example making phone calls in the morning, and then working on major tasks in the afternoon.

Out on the ice, we set up our routine for each day, and even though the weather may have changed or if we were exhausted, there was no requirement to expend extra mental energy deciding how tasks were to be carried out.

The day would begin at around 7 am where two people in the tent would prepare breakfast. This consisted of a hot drink and porridge or muesli, whatever was in the rations for that day. This could take up to two hours, because all the water for cooking had to be melted from snow. Eating the porridge seemed to serve as a signal for the body to want to relieve itself and so people would sporadically leave their tents. Of course, there are not always icebergs to hide behind, so your modesty had to be left at the door of the tent. It was not uncommon to hold a conversation with another team member while you were doing what was necessary, squatting on the ice. We all learnt to go rather quickly, especially in temperatures below –30°C. Once this most important act of the day had been completed, all other tasks seemed easy.

Normally, the lead team would agree the start time for the day, which would be around 10 am. It would take at least 30 minutes to pack up sleeping bags, roll up mats, put on out-door clothing, strike camp, and pack sledges with all the items that had been stored inside. For the first few occasions, this took almost one hour, with clothes being lost between each person's bags and chaos reigning supreme. But gradually over the course of the expedition each person improved how they operated and by the end of the journey we could almost leave only 10 minutes to strike camp, pack sledges and be ready to set off.

Kickstart Tip

> **Routines**
>
> - Establishing a routine can assist in developing a level of order in a chaotic environment.
> - It helps to have some tasks or activities where you know exactly what you have to do and it can lessen anxiety and stress in times of change.
> - Routines can free up the mind to concentrate on other more taxing issues.

Valuing Diversity

Out in the extreme polar environment success is not measured by how much money or what type of job you have, which may be traditional indicators of success in the corporate world, but by how much food you have. Each of us was provided with a bag of daily rations, which were a mixture of snacks designed to help us get energy for the day. These consisted of chocolate bars, pepperoni snacks, peanuts, raisins, and other items that tempted us. It was not the same concoction each day and sometimes an additional Penguin biscuit would be added or a cereal bar, providing a little variety every day.

There were a number of diverse approaches to managing rations that could be described as follows:

The Accountant – This type of person managed their food in a logical way. If we planned to have seven breaks in the day, they would divide their rations equally into seven portions.

The Short termist – The short-term people ate all the good things first. They would get their ration bag for the day, and if there were their favourite items such as the Penguin biscuits or the shortbread fingers, they would eat all these items within the first few breaks, often not having any food at all left for the last breaks in the day. They would then look at other people longingly and hope they would not want to eat all of theirs. This was the category I was in.

The Entrepreneur – Perhaps the most dangerous type of person to have on an expedition. The entrepreneur's approach is to watch what everyone else is up to, and learn what others' particular favourite snacks are. Then they surreptitiously begin to hoard their rations. And just when you would do *anything* to get a Penguin biscuit, suddenly from within their sledge they will produce one and ask what it was worth. From this a type of bartering system developed and one day the highest price paid for one Penguin biscuit was five pepperoni sticks.

What was important was that every approach was acceptable and it's often the same in the workplace. There will undoubtedly be a diversity of approaches in a workplace, and that can bring a richness of experience to a business.

Kickstart Tip

> ### Harnessing diversity
>
> - Teams that are able to leverage the diversity within each individual can benefit from the richness this can bring.
> - Many companies are beginning to recognize that managing diversity effectively will be a key competitive advantage and are taking steps to develop diversity programmes to utilize this opportunity.

The Gender Question

Although Susanna and I were the only two females on the team, it did make a difference to the way the team operated. The males in the group said afterwards that they thought the expedition would be more 'macho' as they put it, and it was actually much more relaxed than they had envisaged. Several of them did acknowledge that they felt this was the result of having a mixed group.

The first hurdle we had to overcome was in the design of the outer layer of clothing. We all had been provided with a one-piece windproof outer layer, which was excellent in avoiding draughts up your back, but hopeless if you were a female and you needed to pee during the day. While wearing a harness round the waist, and numerous layers of undergarments, there was little inclination to undo all of this in the few minutes that we had during each break to relieve ourselves.

Women had obviously not been considered in the design of this garment, and it was not possible to adapt it in a way that could help us. However, the suits were large enough to ensure that the leg zips could be undone from the ankle upwards and then the suit moved far enough to the side to be appropriate! It did become rather uncomfortable at times if you had not tucked in all your underlayers correctly and then there would be another hour of discomfort until the next break, where you could sort it out.

The other interesting behaviour change I noticed was in the level of openness among the group. During the first few days of the journey we were skiing for five or six sessions. On the penultimate or last session my legs would become extremely tired and I would feel exhausted. This meant that all mental energy was used up in just putting one foot in front of the other. On those occasions, if Susanna and I were skiing together, we would acknowledge these feelings, and the conversation would reflect how we were both feeling. 'I am exhausted, and I can't wait until we are finished', I would say. Susanna often would agree, and it was heartening to know that another person was in a similar situation. After all, if we recognized it, then we could both support one another and provide verbal encouragement where needed. During the first few days, if you asked one of the men how they felt, the response was more likely to be 'I'm OK, yes, just fine'. But I could tell by their decreasing stride length that they were tired too. It seemed to be as if there was a level of competition among the men not to admit any weaknesses.

Several days later during the last hour the responses from the men were changing. If I said, 'Oh, I am exhausted, and my legs are agony' then the reply from some of the men would now be 'Yes, so are my legs tired, but we've only got 1 hour to go.' It seemed like their defences were breaking down.

Midway through the trip, it was almost the reverse situation, where now the men were initiating the conversation and asking how others felt in the group. Ironically if this level of openness and trust had been reached earlier in the expedition, it would have helped us to function more effectively as a team. After all, if people, regardless of their sex, are not honest with one another then it can affect the entire team's chances of success. Perhaps a person could really be feeling under the weather or suffering from an injury, and if they continue to over-exert themselves, their body is going to break down or the injury becomes more prevalent, perhaps meaning that the whole team will have to abandon the expedition.

Kickstart Tip

Communication

- It is only when open and honest communication can be established that a team is likely to perform effectively.
- Outdoor team development programmes can be an effective method of achieving this, because a wider range of shared emotions can be often experienced in a short period of time. The key learning comes from effectively reviewing, not just taking part in the activity.

Companies are also continually striving to find new ways to develop enhanced teamworking and more open communication. Companies such as Accenture have recognized the benefits that can be accrued from teams discussing and understanding individuals' strengths and weaknesses much earlier in the team development process. This helps to create mutual understanding and can develop that level of openness that high-performing teams have. It is risky and people have to feel that they are in a trusting environment.

Think about how often you have left a meeting knowing that either you did not say something that you really wanted to or that there was a feeling that something had been left unsaid in the room. Hundreds and thousands of hours must be wasted in the business world because of a lack of openness. It is a risk to be open and honest with people, and you can lay yourself open to attack, but I feel that in the changing style of business that has been developing in recent years, successful organizations are more likely to be the ones who encourage and foster an open environment. This must begin at the top of the organization as the behaviour that is demonstrated here is copied down throughout an organization. NatWest Card Centres, for example, not only state that they value their people, the directors actively seek out feedback from their staff and show that they listen and value what they are told by acting upon it.

Leadership

Our expedition was unique in that it was the first time such a large group of novices had attempted to walk to the Magnetic North Pole. In such an extreme environment, effective leadership was going to be a critical element to the success of the expedition.

David Hempleman-Adams was our leader, an accomplished polar adventurer himself, who had just returned from an arduous trek to the South Pole and had then sailed to the South Magnetic Pole. Helping us was another seasoned adventurer, Geoff Somers, who had been part of an international team that made the longest crossing of Antarctica, covering over 4000 miles in 220 days. The other team leader was Neill Williams, who had been one of David's team-mates from his 1992 expedition to the Geomagnetic North Pole. He had also taken part in several mountaineering expeditions, but had less polar experience than the other two.

David and Geoff had the difficult task of having to lead a group of complete novices in this extreme environment. Another factor that had been difficult at the start of the expedition was the integration of David as the leader, as he had not been involved in any of the expedition's preparations because he had been away on his own expeditions. That task had been left to Jock Wishart, who was responsible for expedition PR and whose brainchild the entire project had been from the outset along with David.

We had developed a good team spirit and even David had commented on his first meeting with all of us that he had felt uncomfortable. He had not felt able to step in and assume the leadership role, as he first had to make sure he would be accepted as the leader of the team. However, out on the ice the situation changed. We were now in an unknown environment and David and Geoff had all the experience.

Autocratic Style

They could have chosen to lead us in an autocratic style. Since they knew everything and we knew nothing, they could just be out in front and we would all follow along behind. It would have meant that we would have got to our goal quickly but our level of individual motivation would be low, because we would not be able to ask questions or learn as we went along.

Democratic Style

They could also have chosen a more open approach involving us all and letting us make mistakes ourselves and step in when there was a safety issue or a matter that required clear leadership. This is the approach they actually used. In my opinion it worked extremely well.

They would enable each group to have responsibility for individual management of each day, and within that process there would always be one of the leaders to raise any important issues, or explain how we should tackle particular problems. If there were more challenging decisions to be made, the leaders would discuss them together.

One example of this was on Day 5, when we woke up to winds of 20 knots and a temperature with a windchill of –50°C. The leaders got together to discuss whether we should attempt to ski that day or stay put until the conditions improved. David was not keen to take us out in these conditions, as we were relatively inexperienced at this stage, and the task of putting up and taking down the tents in these high winds made for a potentially difficult situation. People can get cold very quickly and once the tents are down, there is no shelter. Geoff, on the other hand, did not want to stop, and he felt we should get out there and try. After much discussion, Geoff reluctantly agreed with David, and there we stayed. In this situation, having a clear leader was extremely important, so that someone could make the final decision. Once it had been made, though, Geoff had the grace not to make it obvious that he had disagreed and went along with the final outcome. It was not really the time to be taking chances so early into the trip.

The facilitative and supportive style of leadership of David and Geoff enabled us to get the most out of the expedition. We experimented with different approaches to cooking, laying out the tent interior and other tasks. Sometimes our new ideas worked and other times they did not. Similarly, at West Point the US military cadets are taught that to be an effective leader, you have to give people responsibility early and the opportunity to go out and do things.

Our leaders learnt too. On most of his previous expeditions David had always just cooked his meal in the pot, and then once he had finished his meal he left the pot without cleaning it. The following meal would then be cooked in the same pot. When he suggested this practice to his tent group they were horrified at the prospect of not washing the pots each day. So a new practice began, and after a few days, David said he began to notice the difference. The food actually tasted better! So even leaders can learn . . .

Kickstart Tip

Leadership styles

- A coaching and facilitative style of leadership can encourage people to perform at their best by asking them questions, encouraging involvement and acting as a mentor when required.
- Decisiveness is also required, because at critical moments a leader must make tough, quick decisions and does not always have time to involve everyone.
- Key skills for the leader are being able to ask effective questions and to be able to listen and value the person communicating with them.

In organizations, this approach to leadership is becoming more prevalent, particularly in companies who understand that their people are their greatest asset and they want to get the best from them. This is where the concept of coaching is most effective. Coaching is described in John Whitmore's book *Coaching for Performance* as an interaction to raise a performer's awareness and responsibility, thus helping them to unlock their own potential to maximize their own performance. It is helping them to learn rather than teaching them.

Coaching demands that you recognize that people have more capability within than they are currently expressing and as a coach you can help them to tap into that potential. By asking questions and responding in ways that help the employee to raise their own awareness and generate responsibility, people can begin to feel truly empowered. They own the solutions personally, and they have not been given someone else's solution to address their issue. John Whitmore's book illustrates this approach and shows how beneficial this is to both companies and individuals as a means of helping to improve performance and provide that badly needed job satisfaction.

Learning to Survive with Less

Many companies are now cutting back to reduce costs. Employees often have to provide an improved service or product with fewer resources or less time. The pressure is on to cut corners in order to beat the competition, and this of course can lead to problems later when cracks begin to appear in the level of service being provided.

Recently there was a spate of Internet service providers who began to offer free access to the Internet. They were so oversubscribed that their help-lines were constantly jammed, and their customers began to complain that the level of service they expected was not being delivered. Also, because of the position taken by BT, the Internet service providers were not able to provide unmetered access. When problems do occur, it can often be costly to resolve them. In this case, some of these companies then decided to stop the free service because they could not support it effectively.

In the Arctic environment, the concept of operating in a lean, mean manner also can prevail. When all the equipment necessary for a month's expedition must be carried in your sledge, there is no room for luxuries or items not regarded as necessities. This means limited changes of clothes, minimal toiletry products, items such as versatile penknives that can be used for repair and maintenance, and food and fuel that is measured precisely to ensure that the maximum calorific value can be gained from the least amount of weight carried.

When fuel is limited, the tent does not become very warm inside because it is being used only for cooking. Clothes do not dry and the team must get into their sleeping bags immediately the tent is erected to conserve heat. Luckily for us, our expedition was being resupplied en route and so additional fuel was provided for heating the tents in the evening. It would only take a few minutes before the temperature rose inside the tent. Sometimes it would be warm enough just to sit in your thermal long johns and vest.

In the workplace, people also often have to make do with less. If the economy begins to take a downturn, people are reluctant to spend money and profits may be reduced. As an individual, we could so easily get caught up in our own fears, worrying about how secure our job is or, as a company director, where the next customer will come from. I would challenge anyone faced with having to make do with less to consider the messages that they are telling themselves. We can imagine the worst and worry without thinking about ways to get around the problem. Again fear can take over how we behave as I have described in Chapter 4. We need to be sure that the messages we are telling ourselves are positive ones and not just focusing on the negative aspects of any situation.

Kickstart Tip

Limited resources

When resources are limited be aware of the impact of your inner conversations on your level of motivation. The 'this is hopeless' type of response is unlikely to help you to cope. Try to turn each statement into a positive message to keep focused on what is helpful.

The Mental Mindset

Every day was not always easy on our journey, particularly in terms of the daily physical challenge. Eight hours of continual exercise, which could either be on skis or on foot, takes its toll day after day, and it was sometimes a real test of endurance to keep moving at a reasonable pace for the whole day. When I was not on top form, and lagging behind, I always felt that I was letting my team down by not being able to keep up. However, as the days wore on, it seemed that different people felt good or bad on different days, and there were always others to provide encouragement, or say 'I had a bad day yesterday, I know what it's like.' That support and empathy helped to pull the team closer together.

Another challenge to face was the mental one. The Arctic is a vast, open white landscape almost devoid of life. One might imagine that it is boring, yet I found beauty in its simplicity. Every ridge or mound of ice takes on a unique quality and if I was skiing in front and having to navigate on a particular bearing, I would use a particular ridge to head towards. It becomes the main focus of your attention, and that point is fixed in your head. There is little to distract. Not much sign of wildlife, no noise apart from the conversations between people, or the swish of the skis, and if you are following another person, your eyes focus on the back of their jacket and their sledge in front of your own skis. If you do not concentrate on that and they stop, it's like a domino game, where everyone lands in a heap on the snow.

Because of this lack of mental stimulation, people require an inner mental strength. All these hours with nothing to focus on provide the ideal opportunity for your mind to wander, and thoughts of old friends, or places I had travelled to, events that had passed by years ago, all pop into the mind at different times. It is rare that back in the hustle and bustle of the world we normally live in I can find so much peace and opportunity to let the mind and subconscious freewheel. Some days the results would be amazing. I would suddenly be thinking about a situation that happened years ago, that I had completely forgotten. Yet it had appeared as clear as if it was happening today in my head. This type of mindless thought was much more difficult if the weather conditions were tough. If there was a cold wind, or it was blowing in your face, then all thoughts turned to survival. It seems as if the mind shuts down and only allows enough blood to the brain to perform simple tasks and to think about survival.

During these hours, I focused on ensuring that I could feel all my fingers and toes, and would move them as I skied. If a finger began to lose feeling, then it would take a massive amount of concentration to regain the blood supply. This process is agony as it feels like a million pins are stabbing your finger as it slowly regains feeling. No other issues can be thought about, only the need to feel your finger again.

On other occasions, I would ask myself what I was doing here. Why was I crazy enough to want to ski in this inhospitable world, when it would be easy to be back home in a warm house drinking a cup of tea? This thought must also pass through peoples' minds as they work at their jobs at times.

Kickstart Tip

Mental mindset

- When you question your motivation towards your goal remind yourself *why* you are doing what you are doing. We all need to keep our vision in mind, and our own personal objectives for wanting to undertake any new challenge.
- Find a time in the day to relax and allow your mind to freewheel and not focus on anything in particular.

We were not the only teams attempting to reach the Pole that year. Also out on the ice were a Brazilian, a solo Englishman, a Dutch team, a Swiss team and some Canadians. By the time we received radio reports on Day 14, we heard that all other teams apart from the Canadians had given up for one reason or another. Several had equipment failure, which is a common problem when groups are not sufficiently prepared for the harsh Arctic conditions.

Maintaining Focus

On Day 18 we were expecting our resupply by air, and as we neared the final few hours of that day, we came across a good flat area that would be suitable for the Twin Otter plane. The pilots can land on a relatively short runway, but it must be as flat as possible without pressure ridges. Even if we thought this site was suitable, the pilot would make his own judgement and if it was not safe, then he would seek another suitable spot nearby. Obviously it is easier to get a good view of the ice conditions from the air rather than from our low point on the ice itself.

The next day dawned and it was beautifully sunny with no wind. We were all rather excited at the prospect of the Twin Otter arriving, as it would bring letters from home and some nice treats in the form of food. As the plane flew close towards us we were able to communicate with it by radio, and once it had swooped low and flown in a circle several times, it landed about half a mile away. Immediately we headed for the plane. The pilots did not want to spend much time on the ice in case conditions changed, so there was only time for our base camp person to get out and say a quick hello. Then the items of equipment were passed out to us before the plane took off again, and flew back over our heads.

David had planned for us to swap new tent groups and once we did this and reorganized our new supplies, the day had more or less disappeared. It also served as a good opportunity to rest and regain some of the energy that we would undoubtedly need to see us through to the end.

Kickstart Tip

> ### Recharging your batteries
>
> If the goal that you are trying to achieve is taking a long time to progress, take regular time out. Use this time to review progress, regroup and refocus. Remind yourself of what you have already achieved and give yourself a reward for the progress to date.

The Dangers That May Appear on Your Journey Towards your Goal

Our route was now taking us across a vast area of frozen water known as the MacLean Strait. This meant that we would be out of sight of land for around six days as we crossed it towards Ellef Ringnes Island.

Up to this point we had been walking between islands or on the edge of land, and now we would be totally surrounded by water. It was an eerie feeling to think that all we could see anywhere on the horizon was ice. However, one consolation for us was that we encountered large ice pans, which were easy to ski across, almost like an ice rink back in civilization. When there is an absence of any land to see, it is hard to work out distance in relation to size. So when a dark speck was spotted on the horizon, and we imagined it to be a seal sitting out on the ice, it was possibly around seven or eight miles away. Yet the contrast in colour of its grey skin and the white background made it noticeable.

Later on Day 21 we also saw a dark shape moving on the horizon. This time it did not look dark enough for a seal, yet it was definitely moving. As we moved towards it, we could tell by the way it moved that it was a polar bear. I did not know which part of the team to be in, because half of the team went for the rifles that we carried with us and the other half reached for their cameras!

It was very difficult to tell its size because of the lack of comparison. Once it was closer, we could see its yellowy white coat and black nose. It blended in amazingly well with its icy background and I could easily understand how explorers can be caught unawares as a polar bear lurked towards them. Luckily for us, it seemed to be a young bear, perhaps only 4 feet in length, and there was no sign of its mother. It ambled closer to around 400-metres away and sniffed the air. Polar bears have an amazing sense of smell and can smell their prey up to a distance of 3 miles. It took one look at us, and probably thought that sixteen standing seals in red suits was not what it was looking for, and it wandered off again. We all stood gazing at this great creature of the Polar Regions, marvelling at its strength and size and breathing a sigh of relief that it was not hungry. However, that evening, as on previous evenings, we left a sledge containing some food around 100 metres from the camp so that we would hopefully get some advanced warning if a bear arrived. It was the only sighting of a polar bear that I got on the entire expedition, but I certainly felt vulnerable when there was no fence between it and us as in a zoo.

Being Aware of How Your Behaviour Impacts on Others

When you live closely with people for weeks at a time, no matter how good friends you are, every person has habits that become a little irritating after a while. If you have ever eaten dehydrated food for more than a few days continuously then you will no doubt understand the effect that it has on your body. More than a few noxious gases can be emitted and although our leader Geoff must have experienced this before, he still found it offensive behaviour. He was rather shocked initially when the three of us who were sharing his tent showed no embarrassment and would make some strange noises in front of him. He said nothing for several days, and then obviously felt obliged to raise the subject. He indicated his displeasure at this situation, and so we all sat around and discussed how we could solve the problem.

After a few minutes one person suggested that we make a rule that you could only emit a noxious smell if you were inside your sleeping bag. So we all humbly agreed to this suggestion. Now normally we could sit inside the tent in the evenings, often just in our thermals it was so warm, and after dinner we would chat or write our diaries, then climb into our sleeping bags to sleep around 10 pm. It never got dark, so often it would be quite late before we got to sleep.

It was therefore fairly funny when immediately after dinner that evening one of the team pretended to yawn and said 'Oh, I feel tired, I think I will just get into my sleeping bag'. Two minutes later after climbing inside the bag, he laughed and said, 'Oh, I am not so tired after all', and with a big grin on his face, climbed out letting the emission of a noxious smell leave at the same time. We all creased up with laughter and our leader just looked at us and smiled. He knew that no matter how many rules we put in place, things would not change much. At least we understood how he felt now and could try to make an effort to minimize the instances that may offend him.

In a way this demonstrated how trusting and comfortable we had become in each other's presence. We were now at the stage of an 'effective' team. We all wanted the best for one another, trying to ensure that we worked together and recognized and valued each person's strengths and weaknesses.

In the workplace we also need to be cognisant of how our behaviour impacts on other people. We may be used to listening to the radio at work or talking loudly but this may irritate or distract your colleagues. In addition, when you are trying to achieve goals in your personal life, you may become single-minded. You have to be selfish to a certain extent if you want to move forwards but also be empathic towards others who may be impacted by what you are doing.

Kickstart Tip

> ## Impact of your behaviour on others
>
> - Achieving challenging goals requires being single-minded and focused at times.
> - Notice the impact that your behaviour has on others.
> - If you are not aware then you cannot change. Once you become aware then you have a choice about how to behave.
> - Try to be empathic.

We began to anticipate that achieving our vision was possible. After three weeks of living and working in close proximity to the other team members, with few mishaps, our confidence was raised. It seemed as if nothing could stop us.

Summary

1. Undertaking a small trial or pilot exercise prior to starting towards your goal can provide valuable learning and increase confidence. Even if unsuccessful you can learn a lot. James Dyson had his ideas rejected many times before his vacuum cleaner was put into large-scale production.
2. Use 'what if' questions to help plan ahead and consider all possible things that may impact on your ability to be successful.
3. Attention to detail is critical. It's the smallest issues that can cause failure. Remember it was an iceberg that sank the *Titanic*!
4. Use the knowledge and advice of more experienced people to help you towards your goal. There is no shame in asking for help and other people are often grateful to be involved. This can save you a lot of time.
5. Think big and set challenging goals that will inspire and push you on every day.
6. Some competition is healthy to generate innovation and continuous improvement.

7. In times of continuous change, establish some simple routines such as always stopping to have tea with your colleagues. This can help to bring some order to the chaos.

8. Diversity can provide richness to a team. Seek out and value differences.

9. Once people begin to be open and honest with one another, the benefits will appear and a team will begin to really perform.

10. An effective leader in today's world is able to use an appropriate style of leadership at the right time to get the best from his or her team.

11. We need to work to overcome the fear of surviving with less. It requires us to pay attention to what we are thinking.

12. Be ready to face any dangers on your journey towards your goal by being aware of what is going on around you at the same time. Forewarned is forearmed.

13. Notice the impact that your behaviour has on others. You can then decide whether you want to change it.

Chapter 6

Reaching the Pole

In this chapter we examine:

- Complacency
- Reward and recognition
- Fast-forming teams

There is a tremendous feeling when you begin to see the end of your journey towards your goal. The emotions are lifted and this can encourage you to work even harder or faster as you see the light at the end of the tunnel. In this chapter I consider not only what happens when you achieve your goal, but also how effective teams can be formed quickly to achieve goals in the first place.

Combating Complacency

On Day 26 we began to get a real feeling that the end was in sight. Ellef Ringnes Island was right in front of us and we knew that the Magnetic North Pole was currently located here. As a team we began to feel that we knew how to handle ourselves in this extreme, hostile environment. Our times had significantly reduced for critical activities such as erecting the tent, which had taken at least 10 minutes on the first occasion, and which we could now achieve in less than 5 minutes. We functioned like a team, seamless and often not even needing to talk to one another but just knowing what needed to be done. It seemed that we could be invincible – nothing was going to get in the way of achieving our goal. The anticipation had increased and a new excitement was felt within the group.

David our leader had a favourite catchphrase 'it's not over until the fat lady sings', which was wise advice, as we did not really believe as novices that we could still fail. We did not have the experience of the Arctic that David had and did not know what dangers could lurk behind the next iceberg. In organizations, the same challenges can occur. If a team has been working on a project, and it is successful, then that generates a level of confidence. As that confidence increases, a new danger can raise its ugly head – complacency.

Becoming complacent creates its own pitfalls. That's when a competitor can jump in and introduce a new product to market quicker or better than yours. Competitors look for this weakness and exploit it, so it is important within an organization to keep your eye on the goal, right until it is achieved, never assuming that you can do it without effort.

Think about how many times this happens in sport. An athlete relaxes in a race a little too early before the finishing line, and a competitor, who has determination and is prepared to fight to the end, sneaks in just before the tape to win. This happened to Liz McColgan in the 1998 London Marathon where an athlete beat her almost on the line.

So here we were with 20 miles or so to ski to the Pole. The two Inuits that accompanied us had spotted a caribou the previous day and once we camped for the evening, they went out hunting. Arriving back with their prize it was time for them to enjoy the fruits of their labour. They cooked up a stew and ate heartily. Later that evening they offered some of the stew to each of us.

David who was in our tent declined the offer and advised us to do the same. 'Your body is not used to such rich food,' he explained, 'so if you eat it, your digestion will go crazy'. It seemed too tempting an offer to refuse, as the aroma from the rich, meaty gravy was wafting in the door of the tent. But we listened to David's advice and politely declined, I expect much to the relief of the Inuits who would be able to enjoy more of their stew themselves.

In Neill's tent, they had not heard David's comments, of course, and Neill chose to eat a plateful of this delicious meal himself. Here was the temptation that comes along just before the goal is reached and Neill had succumbed. He was to pay the price the following day. Day 27 dawned and the growing sense of anticipation had increased. However, over in Neill's tent all was not well. Owing to his indulgence in the caribou stew, Neill was paying the price. He looked like death, with a face as pale as the snow itself. His stomach was aching, and he felt weak due to frequent visits 'outside'.

This incident was indeed the type of thing that our leader had warned us against. It meant that we had to reduce the distance we covered that day and the equipment from Neill's sledge was divided among all of us to enable him to try to ski more easily. Even with this benefit, Neill's walking speed was drastically reduced and he stopped at regular intervals during the day. We only had food supplies for 30 days in total and this delay could have cost us the expedition.

Kickstart Tip

Complacency

- Complacency is a big danger. Simple issues can take us aback when we let our guard down and take our focus off the goal.
- Keep motivated and focused on the goal right until you have reached it.

The incident with the stew served to remind us that the fat lady had indeed not yet sung and we ought to remain focused on the goal, even though it was so close.

It was an amazing feeling on the twenty-eighth day out on the ice to know that we would finally reach the Magnetic North Pole. Our team had worked through the phases of team development described in Chapter 4 and was now finally performing at a level that far exceeded even our leader's expectations.

On 13 May we awoke to a fine day. The sun was shining and for the first time on the entire expedition, we had a tailwind. David thought that we ought to decide fairly who would lead the team to the Pole itself. So we put everyone's names in a hat and Andy Higgs, the lawyer in the team, was the lucky man. He then decided to tie the Union Flag onto his ski pole and as we began to ski, one behind another with Andy in front we all felt rather proud and patriotic, even Susanna who is Swedish!

Neill was still feeling a little under the weather, but tried to keep up with the pace of the group, which had slowed owing to a large hill in front of us. Every mile that we skied took us closer to the Pole. The difference today was that we knew this would be the last time we would do this. After five hours, the GPS read 1 mile to go. The air of anticipation and excitement was reaching epic proportions. All the leaders decided to stay back and let us, the novices, reach the Pole first.

Andy then did a countdown as we skied in single file towards achieving our dream. '200 metres, 100 metres . . . I now proclaim that we have reached the Magnetic North Pole', he shouted in an excited manner. It was almost like a train hitting the buffers in a station. We all piled into one another, eager to embrace and share this moment of victory. I could not believe we had made it – 350 miles of skiing across a vast icy landscape had been worth it. As the wave of euphoria swept over us, it was followed by the after-shock of sadness – the realization that our journey had ended.

In business, a similar feeling can occur when a sales target is reached or a project is completed. All those who have had an involvement in reaching the goal are elated, but once the real-ization dawns that the friendship and shared experiences are finished too, then it can bring gloom and despondency. It is worth noting that the enjoyment from such an experience is not just about achieving the goal, but also the process of getting to that point in the first place. Do we go to work only to enjoy reaching our targets or do we enjoy every day at work with the cama-raderie, sharing of good and bad times too?

Kickstart Tip

Satisfaction of achievement

The satisfaction from achieving a goal comes not only from completing it, but also from the highs and lows that we can experience along the way.

Today, as on all other days, we immediately felt that we were not alone out on the ice. Someone 'up there' was watching over us, and had allowed nature to show us its pleasant side on the final day, by providing sunshine and a tailwind. Almost as soon as we had come to the realization that we had made it and completed our journey, the wind suddenly rose and, out of nowhere, it began to get stormy. There was almost no time for photographs or celebration as we worked together to erect the tents for a final time. This was done almost unconsciously as it had become second nature for us to do so.

Recognition and acknowledgement that success is not just about those who achieve the glory was important for the team. We knew that this expedition would not have been possible without our base camp team, sponsors, families and many other people who had helped us along the way. Saying thank you to them and recognizing their role in our success was an integral part of the celebrations. Sometimes as managers or leaders we can forget to do this or be ungracious in the way it is done.

Kickstart Tip

Recognition

- A simple word of thanks is often enough for people to feel recognized for their contribution.
- Don't underestimate the power of a genuine word of thanks to those who deserve it.

Reaching the pinnacle of success is a major milestone for those who achieve their dreams. We all had a feeling of nervousness as we heard the engines from the Twin Otter in the distance, flying towards us. It seemed as if we all knew that the noise meant that people were arriving and, with people, civilization and all that it entails. It would no longer be acceptable to be smelly, have unwashed hair hanging lank on our heads and to carry out practices like peeing in the open air. Our world would suddenly change, and with it the realization that our expedition had ended.

It is amazing how we could survive in our cocooned state, oblivious to what is acceptable in the real world, but each of us accepting the code of conduct and behaviour that we had developed for our icy world, where survival is the greatest issue, and not whether you look or smell good. Priorities had changed, and we knew that they were about to change back.

Fast-forming Teams

This can also be the case in business. Project teams who have worked closely together on a task also create their own environment and identity. Certain words and acronyms can become the common language and when accompanied by knowing looks it is virtually impossible for the outsider to become involved and accepted. It is also why care needs to be taken when changing the members of a team, to ensure that the newcomers can be integrated as easily as possible.

Kickstart Tip

To help with this process of developing fast-forming teams, certain issues need to be addressed. These are:

1. Understanding the culture of the existing team
2. Understanding individuals' strengths and weaknesses
3. Creating a common goal or vision to work towards
4. Addressing the emotional issues, as well as the task issues

In Cisco, for example this process is used to establish teams quickly for a new project where the members may be from different backgrounds and have varying levels of experience.

1. Understanding the Culture of the Team

This is the very nature of how a group of people operates together. It is the 'way we do things around here', the unspoken activities that take place and the values that those in the group have collectively. It can often be like a set of ground rules that those in the team agree to work to and can include items such as how they will behave towards one another, as well as understanding what will and will not be acceptable in terms of behaviour. These issues are noticed when a group states, 'we will encourage people to be open and honest', and then something they do is blatantly different. These types of issue can cause problems, but ultimately if the culture is stated up front, it can make the process of team development easier, because everyone understands and has agreed what the culture will be like.

2. Understanding Individuals' Strengths and Weaknesses

In order to have a highly effective team, a mix of skills and knowledge is required. If everyone wants to be the leader and no one wants to do any work, then it will be quite a challenge and there is likely to be a lot of conflict. Our team worked mostly effectively, because we all clearly knew at the outset what our own and the other members of the team's, strengths and weaknesses were. This helped because we were able to recognize in a stressful situation when a person was likely to be overplaying a strength or struggling because they were weak in a particular area. For example, Julian had a strong gregarious personality, and if a decision was to be made, those who were less vociferous might not get an opportunity to put their views across. But because we were aware of this, we could take steps to ensure that they would also have a chance to contribute.

Weaknesses in particular are important to understand. I found that the men in particular were less keen to state what their weaknesses were, and that perhaps is just a gender issue, where men traditionally have not been encouraged to talk about their weaknesses. In times of stress, which, as you can imagine, are many out on the ice, our weaknesses are likely to appear more quickly and could possibly be to the detriment of the group. Conversely, Susanna and I were reluctant to talk a lot about our strengths, which again could be to the detriment of the group.

Once a team fully understands and accepts the different strengths and weaknesses of each person, then it can function more effectively because each person is more likely to feel valued and accepted by the group. When we feel comfortable within a group, then we are more likely to feel safe to step out of our comfort zone, challenge our capabilities and really improve our own performance and learn.

3. Creating a Common Vision or Goal to Work Towards

Another factor that can help fast-forming teams is having a clear vision or goal. This helps to focus everyone's mind towards the same image and provides the commonality of purpose among the team. Our goal was clearly to reach the Magnetic North Pole – together as a team. All activities that were carried out were all in support of our vision. We all had passion and determination to achieve the goal and ensure that we worked to help one another get there. When one person was tired or feeling ill, the others would rally round and provide encouragement, because they ultimately knew that if that individual held the team back, we would all fail to achieve our goal.

4. Addressing the Softer Issues, As Well As the Task Issues

In team situations, task issues often become the focus for the team. Who will do what, and by what date does it need to be achieved. We were all given tasks during the expedition. It would be either the responsibility for some equipment, or to lead one of the sessions during the day. However, the types of issue most likely to cause failure were not the tasks but the softer 'people' issues. This took the form of conflict between team members, for example the pace that we skied at, or the small, seemingly insignificant issues of camp life. This could be how you looked after your own area within the tent, or behaviour such as emitting noxious fumes as a result of eating dehydrated food for a prolonged period. If these types of issues become frustrating and are not addressed, they can then build and when another problem arises, it is likely that all the other sources of frustration will be included and the person will explode! In order to overcome these potential problems, a coach or facilitator can be used to ensure that these issues are dealt with at the time, and are not left to fester and become bigger problems. Out on our expedition, we had built up a rapport prior to leaving the UK and therefore there was a certain level of openness created and it was acceptable to mention certain sensitive people issues. Whether you are in the business world or on an expedition, addressing team issues is vital, and it can help to ensure that teams perform effectively as quickly as possible.

When the guests stepped off the plane, we were greeted with hugs, champagne and sandwiches. We eagerly accepted everything and soon noticed that the guests were not so impressed with the smells that we were emitting. Having not washed for a month we undoubtedly did not fit into the modern world in this state. It is amazing how people have the capability to adapt to their environment, and as soon as we stepped into the plane, we too could smell how disgusting we were once the heating on the plane had been switched on. Within a few minutes, all I could think of was what that first shower would feel like. How it would feel tingling and refreshing to have the water touch my body and then, of course, how it would be completely unacceptable to put on anything but clean clothes. Our world of survival and basic living was over, and now we were outcasts in the modern world at least until we had taken a long, hot shower.

The expedition ended in a whirlwind with equipment to pack and organize and before we knew it we were about to leave the icy world of the Arctic permanently. It had taken us over six months to prepare to achieve our goals and within three days we would be back home and the whole experience would seem like a dream.

If you have been working towards a goal and have now achieved it, reflect on what you have done, what you have learned and what you will do next.

Summary

1. Complacency is the enemy of success. Once we take our eye off the ball, mistakes can be made or problems may occur. Therefore we need to stay focused until we have completed our goal.
2. Success is about enjoying the journey, not merely getting to the destination.
3. It is vital to recognize everyone who has played a part in your success. A simple thank-you can make them feel valued.
4. Teams that have to be effective quickly are more likely to be successful if they address both the task and people issues at the start of a project.
5. As people we have the capability to adapt to new environments easily, but we need to be flexible in order to do so.

Chapter 7

Been There, Done That, Now What?

In this chapter we examine:

- Ingredients required for success
- Intuition
- Managing failure
- Managing emotions

Once the great high of achieving a goal is over, a great low can follow if there is not another goal or project. In addition, there is an increased level of expectation not only from within yourself to succeed the next time but also from others who will now expect more from you in future. This can be a major hurdle to overcome and it is important to recognize that it exists.

Future Thinking

After we arrived back in the UK after such a demanding expedition, the realization suddenly hit me that it had been pretty exhausting. The media were keen to speak to us and get the scoop on how we had fared on the expedition. Unaccustomed to being in the spotlight, it took me a wee while to learn that you always had to be on your guard as whatever was said could be taken in a different context. Even though all I wanted to do was rest and catch up with my family and friends, I had to respond to the countless media demands. Our story would be news only for a short time then the media would move onto the next story, so in a way we had to capitalize on this situation.

Everyone was eager to learn about how we had survived, and what the Arctic environment was like, but it was tough to find the words to describe the experience accurately to others. We had spent a month looking at nothing, thinking about nothing, and being worried by nothing and it was so unlike 'normal life' that it was hard to put into words.

Most of the others in the expedition team were returning to their families and to the same jobs they had been working on prior to the trip. For several people it had just been another experience to file in their memories and they would go back to their 'normal lives' without it affecting them too much. I, on the other hand, had consciously decided to forgo my career in order to concentrate on preparing and fund-raising for the expedition and now there was nothing much to go back to. I was in the situation of having no job and was not sure what to do next. Having just completed a Masters Degree in Quality Management I did not relish the idea of working on this as I felt there had to be some greater reason for taking part in this experience other than for the fun of it.

This feeling of depression can be experienced sometimes after a major event that changes one's life. In organizations managers need to recognize this just as our manager had done in British Gas all those years ago on my return from Kenya. They need to help individuals to find some opportunities to continue developing.

Companies need always to be thinking ahead and preparing for the next challenge or target prior to completion of the current one. As Ken Blanchard says in his book *Mission Possible*, organizations are operating on two levels. He calls them the current phase and the future phase. While working in the current phase people are focused on the present and are looking for ways to improve in order to achieve present goals. There is also future thinking, which is where managers and staff think about what the organization might be like in the future, who their customers will be and what they will want. Preparation for this future scenario needs to be done in the current phase because if it is not, then by the time tomorrow arrives, competitors have jumped ahead and introduced that new piece of technology or innovative service, which leaves your organization way behind.

It is difficult for large companies to operate like this successfully. Often they are so large that unless they have structures that make it easy for them to change, it is likely that their smaller competitors foresee how the market may change and are able to be more adaptable and better prepared to face the changing times. However, some large companies such as Virgin have done this very successfully because they have had flexible structures that enable their systems, people and operations to change much more quickly. Today's dot.com companies are also successful at rapid change because of the type of environment in which they operate.

Kickstart Tip	**Future thinking** It is important to think about tomorrow's goals today. That way you can stay ahead of the competition and are more able to adapt to changes when they occur.

Taking Control

At this stage after the expedition, I felt I had made that mistake and not prepared in advance for the future. Now that the future *was* the present, I felt helpless. Other colleagues and friends felt that I was capable of doing many different jobs, but as the weeks and months sped by, my confidence evaporated. I hardly dared imagine how I had ever managed to reach the Magnetic North Pole, let alone hold down a challenging job in British Gas prior to that. Every potential job that came along seemed to lack appeal and I began to get confused and not sure exactly what I could do that would be fulfilling and challenging. Instead that little negative voice inside my head was taking control.

I imagined that someone who had heard about my success on the expedition would call up and offer me the job of my dreams. But these thoughts were never going to be reality, and the longer I spent in this state, the more difficult it became to get out of this low. Then one day, I thought to myself. 'No one is going to help you. The only person that can help you . . . is you.' I mulled this over for a few days, and then I began to realize that it was true. I was the only person responsible for being in this situation and now it was about time to get myself out of it. I had to get the positive self-talk back.

It is during these low times in life that it really helps to have some good friends or family that you can talk to, especially those who are positive and supportive and will encourage you without putting their values before your needs. I found it was critical to avoid people who were negative and were averse to taking risks themselves. It's easy to recognize them as these people are likely to drain your energy and generally do not help you to move forward.

In business, the supportive and positive types of people are often good mentors or coaches. They are supportive and do not seek to judge or impose their views on others. They ask questions, and encourage through helping people to focus on what their individual goals are and how they will be able to take actions to try to achieve these goals. I now recognize that these qualities were what I found extremely beneficial in my friends at this time. They knew that I knew deep down I was capable of a lot more than I was currently doing, but just tried to help me find my own way out of it.

Kickstart Tip

Taking control

You are the only person who can take control of the messages you tell yourself. Others can see the impact of them. People can support and encourage but ultimately making a decision to change your thoughts is within only your control.

Eventually, I remembered that Raleigh International, as Operation Raleigh is now known, always needed to have volunteer staff to help run their expeditions. I began to formulate an idea that maybe I could regain some of my confidence by being able to help other people to achieve their dreams in a similar way as I had done all those years ago. I rang them and they sent me details of their forthcoming staff-assessment weekends. I decided to attend one of the weekends in August 1996 and see what role they thought I could be appropriate for. On arrival at the camp I was surprised to find that they were going to assess me for the role of Deputy Expedition Leader. Immediately my confidence level went up a notch or two, as I felt that I must be good at something if they were considering me for the position of being second in command on an expedition which would involve around 120 young people and 30 volunteer staff.

The assessment weekend was much less strenuous than the venturer selection weekend, but there were several team tasks, and the mandatory night exercise, just to keep us all on our toes. The final day gave the assessors an opportunity to see if my leadership skills were good enough as they created a casualty-evacuation scenario involving a large team of people. My job was to coordinate it all and this meant managing 16 people to achieve our objective. In the discussion afterwards I couldn't believe my luck when they suggested that it was likely I would be offered the job as Deputy Expedition Leader on the next Chile expedition leaving in three weeks' time.

I immediately knew this was the right thing to do. It would be a challenge for me to lead such a large group of people in a remote part of the world, and I hoped that it would help to restore some of that confidence that had disappeared. Also there was not much time to sit and mull over this decision. Action had to be taken and equipment had to be organized. I would be leaving to spend over four months in Chile. I now felt that I had found that elusive goal that I had been searching for. Life needed to have a goal and here it was.

The Ingredients for Success

Reflecting back on this stage of my life, I think that there were several things that kept appearing every time I had to decide what to do next. These ingredients I believe can contribute to success both in life or business. Marilyn King, the US Olympian, summarized them as: *Vision, Passion* and *Action*. These are all required in equal proportions.

Vision and Passion

Think about what happens if you have a clear vision and lots of passion, but no action. This leads to frustration. Typically it is seen in people with great ideas, who would be prepared to make the effort to be successful, but for whatever reason are unable to take the action to make it happen. In organizations, this makes people frustrated, as they may know how tasks could be improved to make life easier or improve sales, but because of either perceived barriers or actual bureaucracy they are not able to put their ideas into practice. Typically one might hear statements such as 'No one ever asks me how to improve this job, I could tell them if they only ask'.

Passion and Action

On the other hand, having lots of passion and action with no vision can be illustrated when you see people being really busy but not actually achieving anything. In large organizations, this is sometimes the case, as workers lower down the organization do not understand how their job contributes to the overall vision of the business. Therefore, they carry on doing what they have always done, not realizing that the tasks are not truly contributing to the overall success of the business.

Action and Vision

Finally, the third combination is that of having lots of action and vision, but no passion. Take, for instance, a shopfloor worker who understands clearly that the vision from his supervisor is to manufacture 20 widgets per day. He arrives at work and feels obliged to work because he knows if he does not he will not get paid. However, when the machine breaks down, he has no motivation to fix it quickly or even to think about what made it break down in the first place. He is not really motivated to do this, because it is the company's vision and he had no input into whether it was possible to produce 20 widgets per day. So this reluctance and lack of passion is demonstrated in comments such as 'I knew this would break down because we don't have time to maintain it properly'. In this situation, one way to address this issue would be for the supervisor to sit down with the worker and ask them about possible solutions to the issue. They could discuss whose objective it is, and how it can be achieved in a way where both parties are happy. A solution might be to pay the workers to spend half a day per week on maintenance but the supervisor would be aware of this, and the workers would then try to achieve an output of 25 widgets every other day to compensate. Without the passion from the worker, it is extremely unlikely that this issue would be resolved completely, or it will be done grudgingly and is likely to happen again in the future.

Using your Intuition

Another element that I was now beginning to realize was important in life was listening to my intuition. It was intuition that had helped me make the decision to leave British Gas and work with the United Nations, and it was intuition that was now helping me to decide to leave for Chile.

Intuition is actually our subconscious that is working on a level that we are sometimes aware of but often ignore. It's that feeling that you get when you meet someone and immediately you know there's something about them that perhaps does not correspond to what they are saying.

What is actually happening is that your brain is picking up all the non-verbal signals that are being emitted, and processing them, to give you a feeling. Women seem to be able to tune into their intuition more easily than men, because they have more connectors between the left and right brain. Men have fewer connectors and are therefore able to focus on only one activity at a time. That is why typically if you speak to a man when he is reading the newspaper, he will not hear what you say. His brain is only able to process the information from the newspaper or listen to the person, but not do both at once. This behaviour dates back to the traditional role of the male as a hunter where he needed to stay focused and be single-minded in order to get food for the tribe.

Here is an example. A man and woman who were business partners went into a meeting to sell a product to a distributor. The value of the product had not been discussed between the distributor and the partners prior to this meeting. The partners had, however, sensibly sat down and discussed what they should suggest as their lower and upper limits. These figures were agreed between them at £500 and £750 as a good price for their product in the current market. During the meeting, which was going just as they had expected, the female in the partnership had a feeling that the distributor was impressed with their product and would be prepared to pay much more than the partners had discussed. There had been no mention of money prior to this stage, but the female intuitively sensed that they would need to increase their opening bid. When they begun talking figures the woman calmly stated that the pair were thinking of a sum of around £1000 per item. There was no awkward reaction from the distributor who replied that this seemed just fine and he was happy with that price.

After the meeting, the partners reviewed what had happened and the male said to his partner 'How on earth did you know to state that figure, when we had agreed £750 as our top figure?' The woman had no logical explanation; apart from that she intuitively felt they were thinking about a much higher price. Probably what her brain was processing were all the non-verbal signals being displayed and this would bring her to a conclusion that the message was something different. Her male colleague was only able to pay attention to the words being spoken and his brain could not process all the other non-verbal signals that were being expressed.

This simple example helped this partnership to reap the rewards from the intuitive feeling. And if you think about how often you make a decision based on intuition, then I expect you will find that nine times out of ten, they have been successful decisions. But because we cannot justify it logically, people often dismiss it as a method of decision making.

I believe that as the business world is continually looking for innovative ways to beat the competition, and different approaches to management, working with your intuition will increasingly become recognized as a valuable business tool. Because of the way that men and women's brains are structured, it is possible that women will be able to use this skill more effectively. Therefore organizations need to consider this when creating teams, and use the qualities that women possess as a source of competitive advantage.

Kickstart Tip

Developing your intuition

- Try using your intuition as a decision-making tool and monitor the results you get.
- Ask yourself what you became aware of about the situation that led you to make this particular decision?

Rising to the Next Challenge

Once you have identified another challenge to tackle, you need to try to have the same level of motivation, enthusiasm and commitment to make it a success.

Arriving in Chile, immediately my life changed dramatically again. Expedition life is frenetic, and although I had arrived four weeks before the staff and venturers, there was still a lot of work to do. The expedition leader and I had to find suitable projects to run and to prepare for the arrival of the staff. The expedition was based in Coyhaique, which is Region XI of Chile, and over 750 miles south of the capital, Santiago.

Raleigh International had been operating in the country for 10 years, and had therefore established a fairly permanent field base 20 minutes from town. My role was to organize staff and venturer training prior to them moving out into the field on their projects, plus day-to-day management of the field base. It was a demanding role that began at 7 am and often continued until 10 pm in the evening. However, it was extremely beneficial to experience an expedition from the 'other side' and to be in the shoes of a member of the volunteer staff. It is always a challenge to motivate and encourage volunteers, but it is rewarding when both staff and venturers give positive feedback afterwards.

Chile is a stunning country, with the most diverse landscapes in the world ranging from arid desert in the north to glacial ice caps in the south. Our expedition had projects running in several different locations, ranging from a scientific boating project near the Southern Patagonian Ice Cap to a building project in a forested agricultural area. As Deputy Expedition Leader, one of my roles was to help with the resupply between the three phases of the expedition, as many of the sites were not near any civilization.

One of these journeys took me down to the scientific project located near the glaciated area of the Southern Patagonian Ice Cap. In this area, small icebergs calved into the sea, and as we sailed through them in our inflatable dinghies, it reminded me of Antarctica. I realized that less than six months later, I was now almost at the other end of the world from the Magnetic North Pole. Imagine getting to Antarctica too, I dreamed.

The expedition sped by and my thoughts began to turn to what would be the next goal. This experience had certainly enabled me to regain confidence and there was a great deal of satisfaction in seeing other people realize what they were now capable of, just as I had experienced in Kenya in 1988. Working as a volunteer member of staff had also demonstrated all the hard work that goes into making these expeditions happen in the first place, and how critical it was to be able to motivate and lead the volunteers. Ultimately the quality of the experience that the venturers receive on the expedition depends upon the quality of the volunteer staff who are assessed prior to managing them on the expedition sites. This type of expedition experience could also benefit senior business people who wish to develop their leadership skills in a more demanding environment perhaps than their workplace.

Kickstart Tip

Building upon learning

Once you have managed to be successful in achieving your goal, it is easier sometimes to identify what your next one will be, particularly if they are all in pursuit of a long-term vision. It can be hard to determine what the next step is until you have taken the first one and reviewed what you have learned.

Grasping Opportunities

Throughout this expedition, my sister back in Scotland was keeping in touch with me. One morning, near the end of the expedition, I received a letter from her and enclosed with it was a newspaper cutting describing an expedition that Robert Swan OBE, the first man to walk to the North and South Poles, was organizing to celebrate 50 years of UNESCO.

His idea was to bring together 35 young people from countries all over the world to sail to Antarctica. Robert hoped that these young people would be the leaders of tomorrow in their respective countries. His aim was for them to be inspired by Antarctica's beauty and fragility and go back and spread the word about how it needs to be maintained in such a pristine state when the Antarctic Treaty is renewed in 2041.

This feature was looking for two young people from Scotland aged between 18 and 24 years old who would represent the UK on the expedition. So in her letter, my sister wrote 'I know that you are too old to go on it now, but you just might like to know about it'.

Here was the *opportunity*. Surely if they had all those young people they would need staff to help manage them. This could be the route to get to Antarctica. I was now determined to try to get there one way or another. So I faxed off my details to Robert Swan and thought that this would be the last I heard of it. So imagine my reaction when two weeks later an email arrived from one of his staff saying that they had received the information, and yes, they did need an extra member of staff and was I interested?

This was too good to be true. I could not believe that my wish had come true. Suddenly I would be heading for Antarctica in early January, as soon as this current expedition was over. It had to be a miracle.

Months later, I asked Robert if it had been a miracle. 'Of course not', he said, 'we had two good reasons. The first is that it was a UNESCO expedition, and so someone with United Nations experience was surely going to be useful. Secondly, Geoff Somers from the Magnetic North Pole expedition was part of the team, and he had provided a recommendation.'

Kickstart Tip

> ## Grasping opportunities
>
> - Miracles rarely happen. Opportunities are around us all the time and we need to become aware of them.
> - If we want to grow and develop we need to take some risks in life, not knowing where they will lead.
> - We sometimes have to trust that ultimately the outcome will be beneficial without really knowing why.

It seemed that this expedition was going to be the accumulation of all my previous experience. Here I was going to be helping to lead a group of young people in one of the most uninviting places in the world. My role was going to be even more challenging than the Raleigh expedition because of this extreme environment.

In organizations nowadays this story is equally relevant. People are now embarking on portfolio careers, as opposed to a lifetime in one type of business. This is for two reasons. First, most people no longer have a job for life as organizations change the way they recruit and retain staff. The approach has now moved towards shorter contracts and more flexible roles that offer companies greater diversity should the nature of their business change. People need to be able to adapt to the requirements of the company. For example, as computers and the Internet play an increasingly major part of business, people need to be able to change and update their skills to reflect the changing types of business.

Second, people who have a variety of skills are now more sought after, especially if they can show a track record of success in different environments. Communication skills, the ability to be a self-starter and to be responsible for your own development are necessary in today's business world.

The Power of a Vision

To be able to make the most of each new goal or challenge we face, it is beneficial to add a new dimension of learning or risk to gradually be able to expand our comfort zone. The vision for this Antarctic expedition was powerful and it had inspired me to take the risk and join the team on this journey to the other end of the earth.

The first person from the team I met was the Operations Manager. He was friendly and jovial and I knew from the first moment I met him that we would get on together. I have great respect for Bronco Lane, who was a member of the first British military team to conquer Mount Everest in 1976. That expedition left its mark on Bronco who, as a result, lost all of his toes as well as all fingers on one hand. For most people this would severely limit their activities, but not Bronco. He still runs, cycles and climbs.

The young people were the next to arrive. It was 8 am in the morning when the plane landed from Buenos Aires and 35 lively, motivated and enthusiastic participants appeared in the doorway. They had travelled overnight but this had not seemed to dampen their enthusiasm or energy in the slightest!

There was representation in the group from all over the world. Robert wanted to show that Antarctica was one place where people, regardless of their colour, religion or beliefs, could get on with one another. So he had recruited young people from Bosnia and Serbia; Hong Kong and China; Argentina and Chile; a black and a white person from South Africa; Vietnam and the USA; Russia and Chechnya and so on. Some of them had never seen snow before let alone understand how to survive in it. It was going to be an interesting few weeks ahead.

Bronco had assigned me as a mentor to the young people. Although he had overall responsibility for them he had many, many issues to deal with every day, and so I became the one that befriended them. One of the tasks that Bronco had was to manage the large staff team that had been assembled. This included two people who were producing a film of the expedition, plus a scientist and IT person who would run the web site. So all in all we were quite a large group with diverse skills and experience.

We spent the first few days running a team-building exercise for the Young Explorers (YEs) as the young people were called. This was organized by a company normally based in the UK. Some of the young people could not speak good English so it was a test to ensure that even basic communication was understood! It was amazing how much they all gained from those three days. It was immediately obvious that even though people were from different backgrounds and countries, they were still individuals who wanted to work together.

Kickstart Tip

> ## The power of a vision
>
> If you develop a vision that is powerful enough, people may choose to put aside their cultural, ethnic or gender differences in pursuit of it.

Being an Inspirational Leader

Our leader then flew in to join the group. He had been out on the ice along with two companions journeying from the South Pole to the coast of Antarctica. Because he felt it vital to lead this team, he chose to cut short his journey that had been delayed in starting and join our team. The young people were eager to meet their hero and to find out how he had got on during his journey across the ice. Robert looked exhausted and if I had been him would have immediately jumped back on the helicopter when faced with the 35 enthusiastic faces as he flew in. Nevertheless, Robert took it all in his stride and made time to speak to as many of them as possible. This demonstrated his commitment to the expedition and people were grateful that, although exhausted, he had taken the time to meet them all and welcome them.

Kickstart Tip

> ## Inspirational leadership
>
> - Inspirational leaders motivate their team more by their actions than by their words.
> - They also recognize the value of face-to-face communications and make an effort to do this if they can.

Managing Failure

While all this was going on, Bronco was busy behind the scenes organizing the ship that was due to take us to Antarctica. It was to be the *Professor Khromov* – a Russian ice ship. Bronco had received a phone call that morning from the ship charter company to say that the *Professor Khromov*, currently out on a cruise, had hit a rock and was being taken back to Punta Arenas in Chile for repair. This was a major blow to our plans as it was unclear how long these repairs would take.

It is vital that contingency plans are in place for such occurrences. We now had the prospect of telling the bad news to the 35 young people who were so enthusiastic and focused on getting to Antarctica. This was all they had worked for during the last few months, and it was going to be a great disappointment to them.

The staff all sat down and discussed what we could do in the light of this piece of information. Our leader Robert thought it would be best if we were totally honest with the group and explain what had happened and what we could do as alternatives. The group could also come up with their own ideas and we could make plans according to that. One bonus was that our cameraman was a qualified ship's captain and so he was dispatched to Punta Arenas to be our eyes and ears from the shipyard.

Bronco then got the team of young people together to announce the news. There was consternation that such a thing could happen and although Bronco did try to explain that the repairs could be fixed fairly soon, it did bring an air of gloom to the team. What did work extremely well was the decision to involve the team in planning alternative strategies. We knew what resources were available and so the YEs divided into smaller groups to research what could be done to use the time usefully that had suddenly become available.

In the world of business it is vital that leaders are totally honest with their people. Unfortunately this is often not the case, and employees are left feeling they are the last to know what is going on. Leaders need to get the commitment and buy-in from their team if plans have to change, and in order to get that ownership, the staff need to feel that they have been told the truth (even if it hurts!) and that they have a chance to provide some input. I am sure we can all identify with a situation where a company has been suffering losses, and rather than the leaders asking the staff how they could solve the problems, they announce that they are going to have some job cuts. This can be a knee-jerk reaction and is not always the most appropriate solution.

However, in other companies, they choose to involve their people in making decisions. I know of one large company where this worked. The departmental budgets were to be cut drastically and so the manager of one team got his people together. He announced that this was the case and that he would need their help in resolving this problem. If they could not work together to try to make savings, then staff jobs would have to go. As a result of this approach, the staff suggested several improvements to the way they worked and the department was able to make even more savings than they had anticipated. Yet managers are reluctant to give up control and be totally honest with their staff. It does require a level of trust to exist in the organization anyway, because if it does not, the staff think that the manager is offloading his or her responsibilities onto them.

Kickstart Tip

> ## Managing failure
>
> Honesty is the best policy even if the outcome will be tough. Anyone else involved in your project will respect you in the long term if you keep them involved and communicate openly with them.

In our situation on the expedition, this strategy worked extremely well. The YEs spent the next day providing a list of alternative activities that we could carry out and, of course, they were more committed to doing them because they owned the ideas. Bronco was again scurrying around trying to find alternative accommodation for such a large group in a small place such as Ushuaia as our booking in the hotel was due to finish the following day.

So the next couple of days were spent on moving everyone to new, less expensive accommodation about 30 kilometres out of town, and making arrangements with the YEs to run their series of activities. They ranged from sessions on campcraft and survival in Antarctica to an afternoon of hillwalking and boating. Even though Tierra del Fuego is one of most rugged and dramatic parts of South America and has its own beauty, the YEs thoughts were focused elsewhere and they did not fully appreciate this even as second-best to Antarctica.

Spirits began to dissipate as the delay dragged on. We would receive regular reports from our cameraman in Punta Arenas on the state of the ship but the reality was that it was not going to be in the immediate future. Meanwhile, the young people began to get disillusioned and it was hard to keep up their spirits. During this time, we also had moved to two other hotels as accommodation in Ushuaia became difficult to obtain. People began to get sick, probably either as a result of the mood in the group or the unfamiliar environment.

As explained in Chapter 1, if you look at successful people in business or sport, one of the key qualities that they have is their ability to manage their emotions effectively. Daniel Goleman's book *Emotional Intelligence* recognized that in addition to IQ, a traditional measure of cognitive intelligence, there was another factor measuring emotional intelligence known as EQ. His studies found that successful leaders in organizations were more likely to have high levels of both IQ and EQ.

EQ measures five areas of competence:

1. Self-awareness
2. Self-regulation
3. Empathy
4. Motivation
5. Social skills

Each area of competence is then broken down into smaller segments outlining the behaviours required to be effective. For example, a person displaying a high level of self-regulation would *keep disruptive emotions and impulses in check, maintain standards of honesty and integrity, take responsibility for personal performance and be comfortable with novel ideas, approaches and new information.* Goleman's list offers a way to measure your strengths and pinpoint areas for improvement.

Kickstart Tip

Managing emotions

- There are both internal (in your control) and external (not within your control) factors that affect your emotions.
- Peak performers have high levels of both IQ and EQ and are able to manage their emotions effectively.
- Try not to let outside factors of which you are not in control affect your emotional state.
- Focus on what you can manage and be aware of how these external factors can affect an entire group.

Eventually on 16 January 1997, nine days later than planned, we boarded the *Professor Khromov* to begin our journey to Antarctica. Immediately everyone began to feel more positive and although our itinerary would be cut short we would still be able to reach the largest uninhabited continent in the world and see for ourselves its magic and beauty.

Now I knew that my responsibilities would be different. Here on dry land it had been fairly easy to keep people safe and involved in the activities, but once we were out on the ice and camping overnight, which we planned to do, the whole scenario would be different. People's lives would be at risk and I knew that my knowledge of the ice and survival was not that extensive. Robert, Bronco and myself would be the tent leaders and be responsible for three other young people each. The young people would take it in turns to camp out on the ice with some staying on board the ship and then swapping after a couple of days. That way they could work on the science project and web site while on board the ship, or learn about the Antarctic and how to survive in it on the ice.

First, we had to make the crossing of the Drake Passage, which is renowned for being one of the world's most treacherous seas. It is where the cool waters of the Antarctic meet the warmer waters of the Pacific and consequently it can be very turbulent. Many sailors rounding Cape Horn have written about waves as big as houses appearing from nowhere, and many did not make it at all. It took us three days to cross, during which many people appeared to change colour to a subtle shade of green and there was a distinct lack of bodies present during mealtimes!

Once we sailed into the calmer Le Maire Channel, all of us were captivated by the icebergs and their stunning beauty. It is popularly named 'Kodak' channel after the amount of film that is shot in this area. The entire team was on deck to experience the magic of Antarctica. For me it was quite different from the Arctic. In the Arctic the scenery had been constantly changing as the ice shifted and moved beneath our feet. There had been few mountains or features to recognize and a distinct scarcity of wildlife. Now at the other end of the world, there were jagged mountains sprinkled with snow, giant icebergs moving in the water which itself was a brilliant blue. But the most startling contrast was the abundance of wildlife. Seals, penguins, skuas and whales were all to be seen at different times, and the silence was shattered by the shrieking of birds and penguins who lived in their thousands together in colonies on the ice.

Ironically, although we thought we were the only people visiting, the cruise ships have subtly arranged their timings so that just as your ship leaves a particular beauty spot, the next one sails in. So you never feel that you are in a part of the world invaded by tourists. There are strict codes of practice among the Antarctic tour operators that restrict people leaving anything on the ice or taking anything away. This means that in that part of the world where waste will not deteriorate over time because of the low temperatures, the Antarctic should remain pristine for others in the future.

Our YEs were going to have the experience of camping out on the ice, which is something that most tourists visiting Antarctica do not get a chance to do. We had identified a suitable area just above the British Antarctic Survey hut at Port Lockroy. They were all very excited at the prospect of truly experiencing the Antarctic by living there. Luckily, the expedition had provided everyone with the appropriate outdoors gear as, judging by some of the clothes that people brought, they would not have survived five minutes in freezing temperatures. Hong, one of the YEs who came from Vietnam, had been lucky enough to travel business class thanks to a generous sponsor. She arrived with five large suitcases containing delicacies from Vietnam and enough fashion clothes to kit out a shop but no suitable clothing for living out on the ice! Her clothes were eventually useful at the end of the expedition when the young people arranged a fashion show, and either wore her clothes or designed their own out of paper or other material!

As they proceeded to set up their tents and prepare hot food, there was an air of excitement within the group. The young people recognized that this was a once-in-a-lifetime opportunity and it gave them so much inspiration by seeing the wonders of Antarctica for themselves that they would be able to go back to their respective countries and talk passionately about their experiences.

For me it was also a learning process. Rather than having to be a team member and look to a leader for advice and support as I had done in the Arctic, here the young people I was responsible for looked to me for the same advice and support. I realized that I had learnt a lot on the Magnetic North Pole expedition and could now offer this knowledge to others. Although the temperatures here at –5°C were warm compared to the Arctic, the same principles of looking after yourself like a baby applied. Even if they were going to go out for only a few minutes, it was important to stress to the young people that they needed to be wearing enough clothes and always sunglasses and gloves. In the Antarctic, the problem with ozone depletion is even greater than in the Arctic and it was sensible to wear sun protection at all times.

Communicating Your Message Effectively

The beauty of a place can be extremely inspirational. Our leader recognized that if all these young people were going to be inspired by their experiences, they would have the appropriate skills to be able to communicate that experience effectively when they returned to their respective countries. Once the team returned to Ushuaia at the end of our voyage, the staff team spent four days working with the YEs to develop the appropriate skills. This was a key part of the strategy and a lot of time and effort went into helping them to improve their presentation skills.

The same principle holds in business. If a person has been inspired by an experience or has a great idea that they think would benefit their organization, they must have the appropriate skills to be able to communicate that effectively to those who need to know. That means understanding how people learn, and therefore being able to translate it into the appropriate type of message. Will they be interested in numbers and facts, or will they switch on to the concept and relate to your feelings around the subject? A good idea can sometimes be ignored because it has been poorly communicated. This is why good communication skills are vital in today's business world. Even when we do not communicate face to face and use email, it is still imperative that we consider *how* we are going to be perceived by the receiver.

Kickstart Tip

Communicating your message

- Ensure that you are prepared to communicate your message clearly and concisely.
- Make sure that you use language that your audience can understand and don't be afraid to convey your passion for your goal.
- Consider how the audience might prefer to receive the information. Do they like facts and figures, or an overview, or to get the feel of what you are talking about?

Email is such an easy method of communicating that people tend to write as they would speak, which is in short sentences and gets straight to the point. This does cut out some of the extraneous words that are used to improve a letter, but it can, if we are not careful, lead to misinterpretation of intent. We know that when people communicate, over 50 per cent of what they absorb comes from non-verbal communication and when we email, this vital piece is missing. We need therefore to be twice as careful about what we write to ensure that the receiver gets the appropriate message and with the correct intent.

One of the benefits of email and the Internet is that it certainly makes the world a smaller place. At least 75 per cent of the people participating in our expedition to Antarctica had access to email and as a result friendships that were struck up during the month were maintained easily. This worldwide network of people in different countries has meant that global issues can be discussed on the Internet as and when they arise.

An understanding of the global economy is now also increasingly important. Large multinationals have offices all over the world and expect their staff to have a global awareness and buy into the global vision for the business. Already Accenture have discovered that their teams of consultants working internationally seem to perform more effectively in a shorter time if they invest time and effort upfront in team building. Part of that is for each person to begin to understand the strengths and weaknesses of their colleagues so that they truly can have a high-performing global team. This knowledge could be gained over a long period of time, but they have seen the benefit from doing this early in the project. We also recognized this in

Antarctica and devoted the first three days specifically to team building.

It was now time for reflection and relaxation. Surely all these experiences had some greater meaning and, if so, what was it?

Summary

1. Plan your next goal prior to completing your current one. That way you can maintain motivation and enthusiasm and be more flexible when any situation changes.
2. Your thoughts (either positive or negative) affect your behaviour. Making a decision to change your thoughts is only within your control.
3. There are three key ingredients to success: Vision, Passion and Action.
4. Intuitive thinking can enhance the decisions you make.
5. Find a new area to focus on every time you take on a new challenge. That way it is easier to stay motivated because you are still learning and developing.
6. Opportunities are all around us. The secret is being able to recognize and seize them.
7. A powerful vision can mobilize people from all backgrounds and cultures to put aside their differences and work together towards the goal.
8. Inspirational leaders live their values by showing that actions speak louder than words.
9. Try to be honest – people will respect you for it.

10. Peak performers are able to manage their emotions effectively.
11. It is valuable to consider how you communicate the message about your goals to others. Find a way to convey the passion you have for it and you are more likely to win over people.

Chapter 8

Winning

In this chapter we will examine:

- Different types of intelligence
- Achieving goals

To be able to grow and learn continually we need to reflect on our actions, and then plan a new strategy based on what we have learned. This is called the continuous learning cycle and consists of three elements: *plan*, *do*, *review*. This final chapter addresses the last of these elements and reviews the entire journey of learning from the first expedition at the start of this book until now to find some meaning from all these experiences.

Searching for a Deeper Meaning

Unfortunately I do not learn from my mistakes very quickly, and on my return from Antarctica, I was in an even worse situation than I had been when I returned from the Magnetic North Pole! This time, I had no job, no money, nowhere to stay and had lost touch with many of my friends due to being out of the country for most of the previous year. Where could I go from here? The world was still my oyster, yet I did not see it like that. For once, I craved stability, to be working at a job I enjoyed and to get back to a relatively 'normal' life.

After such a rich and varied life that I had experienced from childhood, I really felt that now was the time to search for the meaning behind it all. I was sure that it was no mistake that I had found the opportunities to work in training and development, to go trekking across icy wildernesses, and to be able to help other people to experience places and take part in projects that changed their lives too. There had to be some greater reason for all this to have taken place.

These days more and more people are searching for meaning in their lives. They are increasingly unsatisfied by material gains such as big houses, fast cars, or a position of power in an organization. Perhaps they work all their lives to be the chairman in a company and as soon as they achieve this, they realize something is still missing. They are beginning to see that there is more to life than all of this, and to be able to find meaning becomes the overriding challenge. If that search is not successful, people feel that their lives are empty and unfulfilled.

By looking for a higher meaning or context in which to put our lives we are tapping into what is now becoming known as our *Spiritual Intelligence*. The book of the same name by Danah Zohar and Ian Marshall states that it does not necessarily have any connection with religion, but more with our ability to make ourselves whole, and to understand what our values are. This level of intelligence has developed from the work by Daniel Goleman on EQ – *Emotional Intelligence*. That type of intelligence is related to our awareness of our own and other people's feelings. Danah Zohar argues that our SQ is like the glue that binds EQ with our IQ or *Intelligence Quotient*, which measures our cognitive intelligence.

For example, you may be working in a high-pressure job in the City where millions of pounds are earned or lost daily on the stock market. If you don't like the job then your IQ would enable you to see logically the advantages and disadvantages – the rational reasons. Your EQ would enable you to have an awareness of how you feel about it, whether you are angry, whether it makes you behave negatively to others etc. But your SQ would help you to ask whether this is the type of environment you want to be in at all. It would enable you to question your own values and discover what your own conscience is really telling you. Perhaps deep down you object to this world of outright capitalism. It allows you to get in touch with your conscience. Looking back to 1997 I now recognize that this is the situation I was in. I was searching to try to understand what my true values were.

Kickstart Tip

Types of intelligence

- IQ – Measure of cognitive intelligence (ability to think and solve problems)
- EQ – Measure of emotional intelligence (ability to recognize and manage emotions)
- SQ – Measure of spiritual intelligence (ability to understand our lives in context of our values)

Finding your Niche

Having had the privilege of working with Robert Swan in Antarctica and hearing him speak I knew why he was a successful international motivational speaker. He was also keen to begin working on a follow-up project to Mission Antarctica and invited me to work with Bronco Lane to carry out a reconnaissance and outline plans for the next adventure. It was during this time that I spent a lot of time chatting to Bronco and trying to work out what would be a good next move in terms of my career. Bronco, a seasoned mountaineer, who has the unique ability to see the best in everyone and every opportunity, was extremely helpful. He knew of my chequered background, and one day I was discussing with him the idea of doing some motivational speaking myself.

I was really looking for something that would make use of all my past business and adventure experiences and I realized that motivational speaking would potentially be a way to achieve this. It would make sense of all the adventure experiences that I had taken part in up until now, and utilizing my business experience at the same time. This was going to be a chance for me to achieve my own potential in a strange kind of way. By helping other people to become inspired through these presentations, it would give me a great sense of personal satisfaction to be able to provide that type of motivation that Margot Wells had given me all those years ago at school when I wanted to improve in athletics.

Achieving Goals

Many things can stop people achieving their own goals. One of these is self-belief. You have to believe that you are capable of achieving your goal. Even if your vision is seemingly unachievable to others, it has to be possible for you. When you encounter a situation like that, when you do not truly believe your goal is possible, or you are having a pang of panic while trying to achieve your dream, one way to overcome this is to remind yourself of past successes. If you can visualize these moments, what it felt like, where it was, and how effortless it was, then the secret is to re-create that moment at a time in the future. This type of visualization is what top athletes use to get 'zoned in' to the appropriate mindset for running a race. If you watch top sprinters in general at the start of a race, they almost close their eyes to visualize running effortlessly up the track. They are concerned only with their own performance and not that of the other competitors. To be able to get into that state and maintain that relaxed feeling is something that top athletes work at. This is because the mental approach to a race is just as important as the physical preparations. When trying to achieve a goal or a vision in other areas of life, a similar focus is required – not to take your eye off the ball, to be aware of competitors but not overawed by them and to run your own race, to ensure you finish first.

As I worked to create a motivational presentation I began to realize that I did have the ability to use my own experiences to inspire others. Eventually the day arrived when the final test had to be taken. Nicky Swan, who was Robert's wife and who had helped him to become a successful speaker, had been working with me for several months. She asked me to present the story to her and although she stressed it was not for her to judge but only to coach me, I felt that if I was given the green light by her I could venture into the world of professional speaking. It was nerve-racking as I think that generally the toughest audience that you will ever have to face are your peers or people who know you. They cannot be fooled by complicated words and stunning slides. They will tell you the honest truth. They will make a judgement about your ability and it's their views that are most important to you. However, after the 30 minute session, Nicky's eyes lit up as she announced that it was excellent and she had been enthralled. This was the seal of approval I needed. I walked out feeling on top of the world. Yet this was only the beginning. It is a long, long road to success in the world of motivational speaking. There are lots of competitors in the business, and you constantly have to improve what you do just as a company would in the corporate business world.

The process of setting up in business as a speaker also helped me to overcome one of my other limiting beliefs. I had always looked at others who were self-employed and thought that they had some special qualities that enabled them to do this, and in my mind it seemed impossible that I would have the skills and qualities necessary to do just that. I imagined that you would need to be an expert in accounting, marketing, sales, administration and IT, not to mention have a passion for whatever type of business you were in. Well, I was correct about having the passion, but, as I was to learn later, as a small business owner skills can be bought in from others, and you should *only do what only you can do*'. No wonder people can work all the hours under the sun when they run their own business. It's not always just to make money, they have a passion for what they do. Otherwise they would not do it.

So being a motivational speaker was to be the way I could realize the dream. I felt that I had now come full circle. My passion is to be able to inspire and motivate other people – in other words, to help them try to use more of their own capabilities, and perhaps undertake a journey to learn more about themselves just as I had done. There was richness in this dream – a passion – and it became my overriding desire.

During any phase of change we can be distracted by others who are negative or who have a fear of risk taking themselves. I learnt that it was best to try to avoid those types of people. Simply spending a few hours in the company of someone who may be your friend but who is unknowingly sabotaging your plans can diminish self-belief. They drain all your enthusiasm and energy and there is a danger that you start to try to answer the questions that they put to you. The most challenging one is always '*how* are you going to achieve that then?'

For people who are setting themselves ambitious goals this is not a question they want to answer, simply because they don't always know the answer. Opportunities come along and things start to happen that then show you the way forward. If the exact answer to how it was going to be achieved were easily identifiable, then it would not be a challenge.

The main thing I had learned on this journey was to become personally powerful in the context of Learned Powerfulness™ outlined in Chapter 1. I had gained a higher level of awareness about what it takes to be successful, plus learnt how to withstand the emotional knocks that I had encountered on the journey. Finally I had come to realize that the only way to be truly happy with myself was to be authentic and to have goals that were fully in alignment with my true values.

Kickstart Tip

Learned powerfulness

Focus – Being able to focus on what you want to achieve in the future and having a high level of awareness
Authenticity – Ensuring your goals are in alignment with your true values and beliefs
Resilience – Ability to withstand the emotional knocks in life

We are all capable of being powerful because we are all born with lots of potential. What does happen is that we listen to what people tell us, or have bad experiences that encourage us not to take risks and empower ourselves to be all that we can be. But it is there – the capability to be personally empowered is within us. So begin the journey yourself to tap into your potential. Everything is out in the world to help you to be even more successful than you already are. There are hundreds of resources available in the form of books, tapes, web sites and people you can speak to in order to get ideas or motivation. I have listed some in this book that may be able to help you too.

As Lao Tse said, 'the journey of a thousand miles begins with the first step' and I hope that by reading this book you have been able to recognize what you need to do, to take your own first step towards whatever you want to achieve. The journey never ends and once you begin on the road to success, your dreams will be bigger and more challenging. But the bottom line is that *you will know* you are capable of achieving them. I wish you well.

Summary

1. The continuous learning cycle involves planning, doing and then reviewing.
2. When we are looking for a higher meaning or context for our lives, we are tapping into what is now becoming known as our 'Spiritual Intelligence'.
3. Visualize your goal and then keep that vision in your head to enable you to overcome resistance from others.
4. Learned Powerfulness is within us all. The challenge is to seek it out and then use that personal empowerment to achieve your goals.

References

Beggs, Alan and Williams, Graham (2000) *Learned Powerfulness Model*, The Human Dimension Ltd, Oxfordshire.

Beggs, Alan and Williams, Graham (2000) *Team Powerfulness Model*, The Human Dimension Ltd, Oxfordshire.

Blanchard, Ken and Waghorn, Terry (1997) *Mission Possible*, McGraw-Hill, New York.

Bolton, Bill and Thompson, John (2000) *Entrepreneurs: Talent, Temperament and Technique*, Butterworth-Heinemann, Oxford.

Coffey, Elizabeth, Thomson, Peninah and Huffington, Clare (1999) *Study into Executive Women Leaders*, The Change Partnership, London.

Goleman, Daniel (1998) *Working with Emotional Intelligence*, Bloomsbury, London.

Hannards, Keith (2001) Grassroots leadership, *Fast Company Magazine*, June, 106–116.

Hemery, David (1991) *Sporting Excellence: What makes a Champion?* Collins Willow, London.

Whitaker, David (1999) *The Spirit of Teams*, The Crowood Press.

Whitmore, John (1997) *Coaching for Performance*, Nicholas Brealey Publishing, London.

Zohar, Danah and Marshall, Ian (2000) *Spiritual Intelligence: the Ultimate Intelligence*, Bloomsbury, London.

Recommended Reading

Allison, Stacy and Carlin, Peter (1995) *Beyond the Limits*, Warner, New York.

Black, Jack (1994) *Mindstore for Personal Development*, HarperCollins, London.

Buzan, Tony (2001) *The Power of Spiritual Intelligence*, HarperCollins, London.

Champy, James and Nohria, Nitin (2001) *The Arc of Ambition: Defining the Leadership Journey*, John Wiley & Sons Ltd, Chichester.

Covey, Stephen R. (1999) *Seven Habits of Highly Effective People*, Simon & Schuster, New York.

De Bono, Edward (2000) *Six Thinking Hats*, Penguin, London.

Doyle, James S. (1999) *The Business Coach*, John Wiley & Sons Ltd, Chichester.

Gibson, Clive; Pratt, Mike, Roberts, Kevin and Weymes, Ed (2000) *Peak Performance*, HarperCollins Business, London.

Handy, Charles (1998) *The Hungry Spirit*, Arrow, London.

Hayhurst, Jim (1999) *The Right Mountain, lessons from Everest on the real meaning of success*, John Wiley & Sons Ltd, Chichester.

Heil, Gary, Bennis, Warren and Stephens, Deborah (2000) *Douglas McGregor Revisited: Managing the human side of the enterprise*, John Wiley & Sons Ltd, Chichester.

Hunt, Rikki and Buzan, Tony (1999) *Creating a Thinking Organization – Groundrules for success*, Gower, Aldeshow.

Jeffers, Susan (1997) *Feel the Fear and Do It Anyway*, Rider, Wisdom Books, Essex.

Jones, Hilary and Gilbert, Frank (2000) *Personal Progress through Positive Thinking*, London House, London.

Katzenbach, Jon R. (2000) *Peak Performance*, Harvard Business School Press, Cambridge, MA.

Lane, Bronco (2000) *Military Mountaineering*, Hayloft, Cumbria.

Lee, Robert and King, Sarah (2000) *Discovering the Leader in You*, John Wiley & Sons Ltd, Chichester

Maslow, Abraham and Lowry, Richard (1998) *Towards a Psychology of Being*, 3rd edition, John Wiley & Sons Ltd, Chichester.

Maslow, Abraham and Stephens, Deborah (2000) *The Maslow Business Reader*, John Wiley & Sons Ltd, Chichester.

Morrell, Margot, Capparell, Stephanie and Shackleton, Alexandra (2001) *Shackleton's Way: Leadership lessons from the great Antarctic explorer*, Nicholas Brealey Publishing, London.

Moxley, Russ S. (1999) *Leadership and Spirit, Breathing new vitality and energy into individuals and organisations*, John Wiley & Sons Ltd, Chichester.

Peterson, Christopher, Maier, Steven F. and Seligman, Martin E. P. (1996) *Learned Helplessness*, Oxford University Press, Oxford.

Timperley, John (2001) *Barefoot on Broken Glass: The five secrets of personal success in a massively changing business world*, Capstone, Oxford.

Robinson, Ken (2001) *Out of their Minds: Making business creativity a way of life*, Capstone, Oxford.

Schwartz, David J. (1979) *The Magic of Thinking Big*, Simon & Schuster, New York.

Thomson, Kevin (2001) *Emotional Capital: Maximising the intangible assets at the heart of brand and business success,* Capstone, Oxford.

Jay, Ros (2001) *Winning Minds: the ultimate book of inspirational business leaders,* Capstone, Oxford.

Weisinger, Hendrie (1997) *Emotional Intelligence at Work: The untapped edge for success,* John Wiley & Sons Ltd, Chichester.

Useful Contacts

Adventures Great and Small
www.great-adventures.com/know/plan/work.html

Adventure Travel
www.adventuretravelabroad.com

North Pole expeditions
Agency VICAAR
Marata 24a
191040 St Petersburg
Russia
Tel (812) 113 27 81
Fax (812) 164 68 18
www.vicaar.spb.ru

BSES Expeditions
Royal Geographical Society
1 Kensington Gore
London SW7 2AR
UK
Tel 020 7591 3141
Fax 020 7591 3140
www.bses.org.uk

BUNAC Working Adventures Worldwide
16 Bowling Green Lane
London EC1R 0QH
Tel 020 7251 3472
Fax 020 7251 0215
www.bunac.org

GAP Activity Projects
GAP House
44 Queen's Road
Reading RG1 4BB
Tel 0118 959 4914
Fax 0118 957 6634
www.gap.org.uk

Geographical Magazine
www.geographical.co.uk/expeditions_travel/

Global Guides for Adventurous Travellers
www.escapemag.com

Mission Antarctica
Crown Street Chambers
2/4 Crown Street
Darlington
County Durham DL1 1RN
UK
Tel 01325 462 041
Fax 01325 462 601
www.missionantarctica.com

Raleigh International
27 Parsons Green Lane
London SW6 4HS
UK
Tel 020 7371 8585
Fax 020 7371 5116
www.raleigh.org.uk

Expedition Advisory Centre
Royal Geographical Society
1 Kensington Gore
London
UK
Tel 020 7591 3030
Fax 020 7591 3031
eac@rgs.org

Tangent Expeditions International
3 Millbeck
New Hutton
Kendal
Cumbria LA8 OBD
UK
Tel 01539 737 757
Fax 01539 737 556
www.tangent-expeditions.co.uk

Travellers Worldwide
www.travellersworldwide.com

Trekforce Expeditions
34 Buckingham Palace Road
London SW1W 0RE
UK
Tel 020 7828 2275
Fax 020 7828 2276
www.trekforce.org.uk

Vacation Work
9 Park End Street
Oxford
OX1 1HJ
UK
Tel 01865 241 978
Fax 01865 790 885
www.vacationwork.co.uk

Venture Scotland
Norton Park
57 Albion Road
Edinburgh
EH7 4QY
UK
Tel 0131 475 2395
Fax 0131 475 2396
www.venturescotland.com

Voluntary Service Overseas
317 Putney Bridge Road
London SW15 2PN
UK
Tel 020 8780 7200
Fax 020 8780 7300
www.vso.org.uk

Index

Accenture 123–4, 184
accountants 119
achievements, goals 147–8, 153, 192–6
actions
    inspirational leaders 174
    success factors 163–4
Antarctic 97, 125, 168–85, 191
anticipation, problems 111–13, 152–3
Arctic 9, 73–153, 180
assault courses 81–2
assessments, self-assessments 56, 74
athletics 9–11, 16, 113, 144, 192–3
authenticity issues, concepts 4, 5–6,
    69–70, 195
autocratic leaders 126
awareness concepts 4–5, 195

BBC 80, 83–6, 106–8
Beggs, Dr Alan 4, 88–93
behavioural impacts 137–9, 148–9, 150,
    152–3
beliefs 3, 97, 192–6
    see also values
    authenticity issues 4, 5–6, 69–70,
        195
    concepts 8–9, 192–6
    messages 8–9
    self-belief 192–6
Ben Starav 58
Bilimoria, Karan 59
Bird's Eye 86
Blanchard, Ken 158
Blyth, Chay 8, 77
body fat 95–6
The Body Shop 42
BP 42
brain power 3–4, 165
    see also mind

breakfast routines 118
British Antarctic Survey 181
British Gas 21–31, 48, 54–65, 116–17,
    158, 160, 164
BT 129
Buchaille Etive Mhor 58
Buchanan, John 23–9, 55
Buenos Aires 172

camels 44–6
campcraft 108–12, 118, 126–7, 130,
    143, 148, 177
Canada 105–6, 112
capabilities 21–49
Cape Horn 180
career plans 13, 171
caribou 144
change 65–70, 194–5
    see also fears
    comfort zones 42–3, 65–6, 73–6,
        189–90
    controls 54, 159–62
    cultures 68–70
    flexibility needs 35–9, 42–5, 54,
        65–7, 159, 171–2
    negative persons 160, 194
    workplaces 54
The Change Partnership 11
childhood 8–11, 12, 75
Chile 162, 165, 167–9
Cisco 150
clothing 121–3, 130, 181–2
coaching
    see also mentors
    concepts 11–13, 32–4, 128–9
Coaching for Performance (Whitmore)
    33–4, 128–9
Cobra Beer 59

codes of conduct 137–8, 148–9
cognitive abilities 7, 16, 178, 190–91
cold temperatures 109–10, 112, 118,
    126–7, 130–33, 181–2
comfort zones 42–3, 65–6, 73–6,
    189–90
commitment concepts 24–8, 55, 60, 69,
    78–9
communications 123–4, 182–5
    concepts 123–4, 182–5
    emails 183–4
    experiences 182–4
    feedback 40, 107, 124
    gender issues 121–3, 151, 165–6
    ideas 183–4
    interpersonal skills 26–7, 79–80, 172,
        182–3
    leaders 128, 174
    networks 24–5
    non-verbal communications 30,
        165–6, 184
    presentation skills 182–4, 191–4
companies
    current phases 158–9
    empowerment issues 176
    future phases 158–9
    harnessed-motivation concepts 55–6
    sponsors 21, 80, 84–7, 92
    values 14–16
competition
    complacency dangers 144–7
    teams 114–17
complacency dangers 143–7
confidence issues 11, 21, 26, 29,
    75–80, 100, 144, 160–62
conflicts 91–2, 137–8, 152–3
contingencies 175–7
continuous improvements 63–4

continuous learning cycles 189
controls
    change 54, 159–62
    success factors 88
cooking 118, 127, 144
coping tactics 32–4
core competencies 38
Cornwallis Island 114
Coyhaique, Chile 167
Croatia 63, 66–70
cultures
    change 68–70
    fast-forming teams 149–50
current phases, organizations 158–9
customer needs 37–8

Daily Telegraph 63
dangers, goals 135–6
decision making
    intuition 62–5, 167
    leaders 128
dehydrated foods 137
democratic leaders 126–9
depression 158–60, 177–8
details 111
determined attitudes 79
development stages
    exercises 94–6
    mental strength 96–8, 131–5
    teams 88–93, 146, 149–53, 184
dicts 96
diversity benefits
    concepts 120–21
    teams 40–42, 119–21, 173–4
dot.coms 38–9, 159
Drake Passage 180
dynamic teams 89, 90, 93
dysfunctional teams 90, 91–2

economic restraints 129–31
effective teams 90, 92–3, 138, 143
elastic cords 111–12
Elephant Island 97

Ellef Ringnes Island 114, 135, 143
emails 183–4
    see also Internet
embryonic teams 89–90
emergent teams 90, 92
emotions 4–7, 16, 30, 89, 93, 99–100,
    143, 178–80, 190
empathetic behaviour 138, 178–9
empowerment issues 4, 14–16, 126–9,
    176, 195–6
encouragement benefits 9–13
energetic approaches 3–4, 115
enjoyment benefits 77–8
enthusiastic attitudes 3–4, 25–8, 41–2,
    79, 115, 172
entrepreneurs 24–5, 59, 120
environmental issues 42
Everest 8, 172
exercises 94–6, 107–8, 131
experiences, communications 182–4
experts 108, 111–13, 125, 143–6

facilitators 41, 127–8, 152–3
failures 143–4, 175–7
fast-forming teams 149–53
fat 95–6
fears 31–4, 65–7, 76, 97–100, 130
    concepts 32–4, 65–7, 97–100
    coping tactics 32–4
    what-if scenarios 98–100
Federal Express 37
feedback 40, 107, 124
fitness factors 94–6
flexibility needs
    change 35–9, 42–5, 54, 65–7, 159
    concepts 36–9, 171–2
    Internet 171
focus issues, concepts 4–5, 29, 67, 100,
    132–5, 145–6, 193–6
food 96, 118, 119–21, 127, 130, 136–7,
    144–5
former Yugoslavia 5, 63–70
forming phase, teams 89

friends 160–61, 194
frostnip dangers 110, 132–3
fuel considerations 130
fund-raising activities 29–30, 74, 83–4
future achievements 4–5, 67, 195
future goals 29, 153, 157–9, 168–9
future phases, organizations 158–9

gender issues 121–3, 151, 165–6
    communications 121–3, 151, 165–6
    intuition 165–7
    non-verbal communications 165–7
    stereotypes 165–7
General Electric 37
Glencoe 57–8
Global Positioning System (GPS)
    115–16, 146
globalization 184
gluttonous diets 96
goals 3, 105, 113–17, 133–6, 146–7,
    192–6
    achievement satisfaction 147–8, 153,
        192–6
    authenticity issues 4, 5–6, 69–70,
        195
    complacency dangers 143–7
    completion euphoria 146–8, 153, 157
    concepts 113–17, 133–6, 143, 151–2,
        157, 192–6
    dangers 135–6
    future goals 29, 153, 157–9, 168–9
    GROW model 34
    journey's end 146–8, 153, 157, 196
    milestones 114–16, 195–6
    next goals 29, 153, 157–9, 168–9
    setting goals 113–17, 151–2
    values 4, 5–6, 68–70
Goleman, Daniel 6–7, 89, 100, 178,
    190
GPS *see* Global Positioning System
GROW model 33–4
Gunnell, Sally 113
gym sessions 94–5

habits 137–8, 148, 152–3
harnessed-motivation concepts 55–6
helping-other-people considerations 56–62
Hemery, David 10
Hempleman-Adams, David 80–81, 94–6, 112, 114–15, 125–7, 143–6
Higgs, Andy 146
Hillary, Sir Edmund 8, 77
hobbies 57
honesty issues 122–4, 150, 177
The Human Dimension (Beggs) 88
humour 79
Hunter, Tom 59

ice landscapes 135–6, 168, 180
ideas 57–61, 183–4
individuals
 behavioural impacts 137–9, 148–9, 150, 152–3
 teams 116–17, 124, 150–51
inertia 33
information benefits, risks 24–5
information technology (IT), rapid changes 37
injuries 123, 172
inspirational leaders 174
intelligence quotient 190–91
internal blockages 76
Internet
 dot.coms 38–9, 159
 emails 183–4
 flexibility needs 171
 service providers 129
interpersonal skills 26–7, 79, 172, 182–3
intuition
 concepts 164–7
 decision making 62–5, 167
 gender stereotypes 165–7
IT *see* information technology

jobs
 for life 13, 171
 satisfaction 129
journey's end 146–8, 153, 157, 196

Kenya 35–48, 158, 168
King, Marilyn 162–3
knowledge
 experts 111–13, 125, 143–6
 teams 150–51
'Kodak' channel 180

Lake Baringo, Kenya 46–8
Lane, Bronco 172–5, 179, 191–2
Lao Tse 196
Le Maire Channel 180
leaders 11, 27, 40–41, 43, 108, 111–13, 124–9, 161–2
 actions 174
 communications 128, 174
 concepts 124–9, 174
 decision making 128
 inspirational leaders 174
 learning 127–8
 listening skills 128
 selection methods 161–2
 styles 126–9
Learned Powerfulness concepts 4, 69, 93, 195–6
learning 43, 57, 70, 75–7, 123, 169
 continuous cycles 189
 integration concepts 53–4, 62
 leaders 127–8
 reviews 189–96
listening skills, leaders 128
local communities 28, 58
London Marathon 144

Macarthur, Ellen 6, 8
McColgan, Liz 144
MacLean Strait 114, 135
Magnetic North Pole 9, 73–153, 160, 170, 182

Marshall, Ian 190
Marshall, Simon 82
Maslow's needs 88–90
Matthews Peak, Kenya 44–6
meaning 189–91
Mears, Ray 97
media 80, 83–6, 106–8, 157
meetings 124
men *see* gender issues
mental strength 7, 16, 96–8, 131–5, 178
 see also mind
mentors 11–13, 16, 43, 173
 see also coaching
 concepts 11–13, 32–4, 128
 fears 32–3
 GROW model 33–4
Merrill Lynch 14
messages, beliefs 8–9
milestones 114–16, 195–6
mind
 brain power 3–4, 165
 cognitive abilities 7, 16, 178, 190–91
 emotions 4–7, 16, 30, 89, 93, 99–100, 143, 178–80, 190
 games 96–8, 131–5
 gender stereotypes 165–7
 mental strength 7, 16, 96–8, 131–5, 178
 subconscious mind 3, 70, 75, 165
miracles 170–71
Mission Possible (Blanchard) 158
mistakes 189
Mitchell, Richard 81
motivating factors 76–7
motivational speakers 191–4
Mount Everest 8, 172
muesli 118
multinationals 184

NatWest Card Centres 124
needs 88–93
negative motivation issues 77–8, 100, 160, 194

networks 24–5
Noice Peninsula 114
non-verbal communications
    gender stereotypes 165–7
    generalizations 30, 165–6, 184
normal lives 158, 189–90
norming phase, teams 89
Magnetic North Pole 9, 73–153, 160,
    170, 182
noxious-smells etiquette 137–8, 148,
    152–3

openness issues 122–4, 150, 153, 177
Operation Raleigh 21–49, 57–8, 61, 74,
    78, 161–2
    see also Raleigh International
opportunities 9, 14, 16, 22–4, 64, 80,
    158, 169–72
options, GROW model 34
organizations
    see also companies
    current/future phases 158–9
Oxfam 42
ozone layer 182

pack sizes 129–30
parallel processing, gender stereotypes
    165–6
passions 24–8, 29–32, 60–62
    concepts 24, 29–32, 163–4
    demonstrations 30–31
    self-employed persons 194
    success factors 163–4
past successes 192–3
peak-performance issues
    concepts 4–7, 89, 93, 100, 146
    elements 4–7, 179
Penguin biscuits 119–20
penguins 180
performance enhancements
    peak-performance issues 4–7, 89, 93,
        100, 146, 179
    teams 41–2, 45, 89, 93

The Performance Group 37
performing phase, teams 89
photocopiers 110
physical fitness factors 94–6
Piercy, Mike 82
plane landings 134, 148
plans 13, 34–6, 87–8, 109–10,
    175–7
polar bears 136
polar plod 115
Polaris Mine 114
porridge 118
Port Lockroy 181
portfolio careers 171–2
positive thinking 97–8, 160–61, 194
preparations 34–6, 87–8, 95, 98–100,
    109–10, 133
presentation skills 182–4, 191–4
proactive approaches 9
problems, anticipation 111–13, 152–3
Professor Khromov 175, 179
Punta Arenas 175

qualities, self-assessments 56

Raleigh International 161–2, 167–9
    see also Operation Raleigh
reality 31–2, 34
recognition issues 148–9
recruitment criteria 79–80
reflective practices 153, 189–96
relatives 160
relaxation benefits 133–4, 185
resilience issues, concepts 4, 6–7, 35,
    195
Resolute Bay, Canada 105–6, 112
resources 129–31, 196
responsibilities 13, 16, 34
    self-development issues 172
    social responsibilities 42
reviews, learning 189–96
The Ridgeway 81–2
rifles 136

risks
    concepts 24–5, 80–81, 194–6
    information benefits 24–5
role models 10–11
    value 10–11
routines 117–19, 168
running benefits 94–5

Sandhurst 81
Santiago 167
seals 135–6, 180
selection methods
    leaders 161–2
    teams 23–8, 79–83, 162
self-actualization needs 89–90
self-assessments 56, 74
self-awareness competencies 178–9
self-belief 192–6
self-development issues 172
self-employed persons 194
self-esteem issues 11, 76, 85, 89–90
self-regulation competencies 178–9
self-starters 172
selfishness 40
Shackleton, Ernest 97
Shell 42
short termists 120
sickness 145, 178
skiing activities 94–5, 97, 107–10,
    126–7, 131–6, 146
skills 4–5, 26–7, 57, 79–80, 128,
    150–51, 172, 182–3, 191–4
skuas 180
sledges 107–8, 118, 120, 129–30, 136
smelly habits 137–8, 148, 152–3
social issues
    needs 89–90
    responsibilities 42
    soft skills 152–3
soft issues 152–3
Somers, Geoff 125–7, 137, 170
South Pole 97, 125, 168–85, 191
Southern Patagonia Ice Cap 168

speakers 191–4
The Spirit of Teams (Whitaker) 76
spiritual intelligence 190–91
sponsors 21, 80, 84–7, 92, 148
sprinters 192–3
stability cravings 189–90
  see also comfort zones
status needs 89–90
storming phase, teams 89
strengths 91, 96–8, 124, 131–5,
  150–51, 184
subconscious mind 3, 70, 75,
  165
  see also mind
success factors
  actions 163–4
  controls 88
  ingredients 162–4
  passion 163–4
  past successes 192–3
  recognition 148–9
  vision 163–4, 172–4
sunglasses 182
survival techniques, flexibility needs
  35–9, 96–7, 159, 171–2
Swan, Nicky 193
Swan, Robert, OBE 169–70, 173–6,
  179, 191, 193
swimming benefits 94–5

Team Powerfulness concepts 88–93
teams 21–49, 74, 79–83, 88–93,
  114–17, 121–4, 184
  behavioural impacts 137–9, 148–9,
    150, 152–3
  competition benefits 114–17
  concepts 39–42, 45, 79–83, 88–93,
    114–17, 121–4, 149–53, 184
  conflicts 91–2, 137–8, 152–3
  cultures 149–50
  development stages 88–93, 146,
    149–53, 184

diversity benefits 40–42, 119–21,
  173–4
familiarity problems 137–8, 152–3
fast-forming teams 149–53
gender issues 121–3, 151
globalization 184
'goodbye' processes 85
individuals 116–17, 124,
  150–51
performance enhancements 41–2,
  45, 89, 93, 146
selection methods 23–8, 79–83, 162
soft issues 152–3
what-if scenarios 98–100
television 80
temperatures 109–10, 112, 118, 126–7,
  130–33, 181–2
tents 108–12, 118, 126–7, 130, 137,
  143, 148
tests 21–49, 107–8
thanks 148
Tierra del Fuego 177
time-management skills 4–5
tiredness 122–3, 131
Titanic 139
Tito 63
toilets 118, 121–2
total quality management 63
tour operators 180–81
trainers 55–6
trust 99–100, 123, 138, 171
Tuckman's team model 89
Twin Otter planes 134, 148

'Ultimate Challenge' expedition
  73–153
United Nations 5, 63–70, 165, 169–70

values
  see also beliefs
  authenticity issues 4, 5–6, 69–70, 195
  companies 14–16

Venture Scotland 60–61
Virgin 159
vision 57–61, 67, 88, 96, 117,
  133, 139, 151–2
  concepts 163–4, 172–4,
    192–3
  success factors 163–4, 172–4
visualizations, past successes
  192–3
voluntary work 60–62, 162, 165,
  167–9

Wal-Mart 38
walks 81–2, 114–17, 177
Ward, Hugh 81
weaknesses 91, 124, 150–51,
  184
Wells, Allan 9
Wells, Margot 9, 11, 16, 192
West Point, USA 127
whales 180
what-if scenarios 98–100, 109
Whitaker, David 76
Whitmore, John 33–4, 128–9
Wikman, Susanna 82
will 34
Williams, Graham 4
Williams, Neill 80–81, 125,
  145–6
windchill factors 126–7
winning 189–96
Wishart, Jock 80–85, 125
women *see* gender issues
*Working with Emotional
  Intelligence* (Goleman) 6–7,
  178, 190
workplaces, change 54

former Yugoslavia 5, 63–70

Zagreb 66–70
Zohar, Danah 190